F*CK IT, WATCH THIS

F*CK IT, WATCH THIS

SAYING THE QUIET PARTS OUT LOUD

ANA VISNESKI

MANUSCRIPTS
PRESS

F*CK IT, WATCH THIS

Saying the Quiet Parts Out Loud

ISBN   979-8-88504-398-4   *Paperback*

979-8-88504-399-1   *Hardcover*

979-8-88504-397-7   *Ebook*

To my husband, Eric. Without you, this book would never have been written. Thank you for all your love and support.

To my Coast Guard family, especially the PA family, I wouldn't be who I am today without you. Thank you for all you have taught me.

Contents

Introduction

Hi! You likely picked up this book to take a peek for a reason. Either you are a supporter of the Coast Guard or because you are looking for a different kind of leadership book, or you liked the cover. Or you are my mom or a friend who has bought a copy before reading how much I swear in here. All of these are great reasons. This book is for you.

All our lives, we are told there are rules we need to play by, lessons we need to learn, and that there is a path to success. We are told we need to not only go to college but what to study. We are told our career has to have a certain path, check those boxes; to be a hard worker and be good at what we do, but don't stand out, don't speak up against those with rank.

Think back to the first time you remember someone getting a promotion as an example of winning. When you started in the corporate world, who taught you how to be a leader? You don't always glean these things from a book but a lot of times simply by being in the system, observing what is going on around you, and imitating what you see others doing that you think is right, or straight up what they tell you is right.

Not only does that suck for you professionally, because it is limiting, but it can suck for your soul.

It's time to take a step back at what you have considered normal, how you have been playing the career game, and realize that in fact, you get to be the game master of your own story.

This book is going to piss a fair number of people off. I mean, some bits will probably irritate everyone, but I am pretty sure, cover to cover, a lot of admirals and captains in the Coast Guard are going to have some words for me about my opinions of the Coast Guard.

I learned as many things from the Coast Guard's fuck-ups as I did from the successes. An unwritten rule is thou shalt not disparage the noble service. Well. Considering this book is about learning the system you worked in and how to find your own way to do things within that system, you can expect that I am not so great at following rules.

I wouldn't be where I am today without the service and my Coast Guard family. So, to those admirals and captains—or other Coasties—who picked up this book, fair warning. I love the Coast Guard the same way I love my family, with full acknowledgment of its flaws.

The second group I expect won't be pleased with me are the executive traditionalists—the ones who believe there is a specific path to make vice president, or otherwise succeed, and anyone who does it another way doesn't deserve to be there. I wish I could say those folks don't exist, but they definitely do.

I am sure you know the type. The type who will tell you what you want to hear but then turn around and do whatever makes them look good; the ones who give hand-waving political answers instead of being to the point and honest; the type of guys who think The Wolf of Wall Street is a how-to documentary and not a cautionary tale.

This book will also show you how to make yourself resilient and adaptable—to have infinite paths to success because you have learned how to *make* the game instead of simply play it. I got sick of the leadership books that are all fluffy prose with no actionable items to help you *make* changes or try new things. This book aims to give you clear actionable things to do or questions to ask yourself, to become the leader you want to be.

This whole book is a "fuck that!" to societally pressured behavior or patterns of thinking; a big old *nope* to so many of the things we are "taught" both in the military and corporate settings. I am a strong believer that, to succeed in life and the world, you need to be willing to look at the rules and go "Pfft, I can do better than this." Then set up your own win parameters and set about taking the world on.

My mother tells a story about when I was a baby—well, two stories, but the one about how my first phrase was "You asshole!" isn't quite applicable here. The way she tells it, I refused to walk because I knew someone would pick me up, and also refused to crawl on grass because I didn't like the way it felt on my hands.

So, my mom used to be able to set me on a blanket in the park and know I wasn't going anywhere. Well, I wasn't until one day I saw the other kids playing in a sprinkler and wanted to join them. Mom wouldn't carry me, so I got up and walked to play with the other kids. She says I have continued to live my life that way—not taking a single first step, just getting up and walking toward my goal.

Being selectively stubborn, as it turns out, has served me well—as has straight up throwing myself into the unexpected. When I decided to go to Officer Candidate School for the Coast Guard in 2004, many of my friends were stunned; I was too liberal to go into the military; I thwarted rules any chance I got without ever technically breaking them; I was simply too *me*.

As a third generation Coastie, I had a pretty good idea what I was getting into. I knew I would have to learn to conform, that I would have to learn how to at least look like I was following the rules. I viewed it as an adventure and a game, and you can't play if you don't join in.

That doesn't mean I didn't take my career seriously. I took it very seriously, just not in the way my mentors, commanding officers, or parents thought I should. To everyone else, success in the service looked like getting that next promotion and making it to captain or admiral. I said from day one I could care less about how much gold I got on my shoulders. I wanted to do the things that challenged me, which meant I took jobs that weren't "good for my career" in the making-captain sense—causing no end of frustration for some well-meaning senior officers.

I wanted to do the things that made an impact, like starting the Coast Guard Social Media program. I wanted to do the things that straight up felt like what I should be doing. Turns out that would put me in direct opposition to what the Coast Guard thought I should be doing to get promoted. *Oops.*

Spoiler alert, I didn't make captain. Hell, I got passed over from O3–O4, which I will admit was bittersweet. Why? Because I had gotten a call from the International Trade Administration offering me a GS15 role. For those of you blessedly unaware of the leveling of US government employees, this is roughly the equivalent of a captain in the Coast Guard. That's right, the very same week I got passed over for O4, I was offered a role that was a 3-level jump. And jump I did…

It wasn't until I made vice president at one of the biggest tech companies in the world, six years after leaving the service, that I realized I learned a lot more from the Coast Guard than I thought, and most of the lessons weren't what the service set out to teach me.

For seventeen weeks of Officer Candidate School, you learn everything from the Nautical Rules of the Road, how to hold your fork in a dignified manner, to how to do basic firefighting. You go through a ton of leadership classes, learning how to work with personality types and how to lead during times of high stress. Once you become an officer overseeing a team, unlike when you go from being an individual contributor (IC) at a company to a manager, you get additional training for the type of roles you take on.

I wish corporate America would get on board with consistent leadership training—not getting their new managers training but continuing to provide management and leadership training to personnel as they grow. Let's be honest, most of the poor leaders I have met or worked for could have done with a class or twelve teaching them the basics of how not to be a douche canoe. A few lessons on how to be empathetic to those who are different than you might not have gone amiss either. There is a reason there is a huge market for executive coaches.

So, yes, there is a lot of tactical training, as well as other types of training, you go through every year in the Coast Guard. Sure, there are plenty of things the Coast Guard taught me through years of leadership and management training, through pepper spray training—have milk on hand whenever dealing with peppers—and the various communications trainings. Yes, those things have come in handy.

All that said, the most important lessons were the off-the-wall ones. The way to process and triage, and the way to be strategically stubborn and get the mission done, even when those around me thought it was crazy. I have found as I am leading my teams, or mentoring others, some of the examples I use are not the ones I learned in any of the leadership classes or ones I was *officially* taught. Plenty of books are out there on the leadership style any various service teaches you. This one here aims to give you the lessons they maybe aren't so proud of having unintentionally taught.

But, Ana, you say, dear reader, *you didn't make admiral. Hell, you got passed over at a pretty junior level. Why should I listen to you?* Well, first of all, you should only ever listen to that voice inside yourself that tells you what is true for you. The thing is, you should educate that voice with as many different views as possible. This book is probably not the book if you are looking for advice on how to make admiral; there are lots of books already for that. Here is where I show you how to use a system like the Coast Guard—or any major corporation—to get what you need in order to get to where you want to be.

No, I didn't make O6, but within six years of getting out of the Coast Guard, I landed a role as a vice president at one of the biggest tech companies in the world, without giving up who I am—tattoos, sass, and all. More importantly, I have accomplished what others—often those with more experience than me—have deemed "impossible" at high-intensity companies like AWS. I did this while maintaining high morale on my teams and minimizing burnout. I did all these things, both in and since the Coast Guard, eschewing some of the more traditional hierarchical methods of leadership and engagement. Stick that in your promotion board pipe and smoke it, promotion board.

CHAPTER 1

Play Your Own Way

"Just Play. Have Fun. Enjoy the game."

—MICHAEL JORDAN

Before we get into the sea stories, it is important to understand a specific approach I use to pretty much anything I do. I look at things as a kind of game, a system with rules you have to play by. This key methodology has helped me look at challenges as not a roadblock or the end of an idea but a chance to make my brain do gymnastics and tackle the impossible problems.

As I mentioned in the intro, my friends were all shocked when I decided to join the Coast Guard. Scratch that, I should say they were shocked when I decided to join the Coast Guard again. I had left the Academy—which is technically harder to get into than an Ivy League school, sorry not sorry Harvard—at seventeen, much to the chagrin of my family.

Now, here I was five years later turning around and going back at it. This time, I had been accepted into Officer

Candidate School (OCS) a little over a year after I graduated from the University of Washington. I had gone to a civilian school, studied abroad in the UK, and moved to Antarctica for a bit after I graduated, but now it was time to get started on a career.

My friends thought I was insane. I was outspoken, artistic, liberal, and generally known for being the one in the group who loved to find ways to get around the rules without ever breaking them. The Coast Guard was where I wanted to go because a desk job like I saw them settling into seemed like a slow death. I wanted an adventure.

"What better way to play the game than get inside and mess with the rules?" I told my best friend. Little did I know that would be the statement that would define my career.

In gaming, there is a term called metagaming. Now, in the world of tabletop roleplay games, or live-action roleplay games, the term metagaming means using your real-life knowledge concerning a game to determine your character's actions, even when your character in the game has no reason to know the information you are supplying from your real-world knowledge. Outside of Table Top Role Play games (TTRPGS)—think Dungeons & Dragons—metagaming usually means using knowledge of external factors to gain an advantage in the competition.

Metagaming breaks the game in most cases and is generally frowned upon. I am taking the meaning of metagaming a step further, and to not only use the knowledge of external factors to get an advantage over the competition but to actually recognize the rules of the game and, while never breaking them, play the game to your own set of rules, specifically redefining what the rules outline as winning to what you personally define as winning. There is winning the game the way it was designed and then there is winning that accomplishes what you want.

PLAYING BATTLETECH CHICKEN

When I was in college, I worked at the Wizards of the Coast Game Center on University Avenue near the University of Washington. At the game center, there were these massive pill-shaped boxes called BattleTech Pods. BattleTech started as a tabletop RPG and is largely considered one of the oldest TTRPGs around, having launched in 1984.

In 1990, a company called Virtual World turned these games into full-on interactive video games, where you would climb inside one of the pods and find yourself in what looked like the cockpit of one of the giant walking war machines—a battlemech. (For their time, they were incredible, and to be honest, they hold up pretty well today.) A league was around this game, where people would play for the leaderboard ranks. A player could even become a Mech Master, by racking up a certain number of points, number of hours, and then run a gauntlet test against the current Masters.

Very few women played. A lot of attention and pressure was put on us to become "Masters"—a pressure I staunchly refused to give in to. Instead, I started making up my own game. I always chose the smallest, fastest mech, a mech called the Owens. In the field, the mech was half the height of all the others, and had almost no armor. Heck, the weapons on it kind of sucked too, but what it did have was speed. While everyone was trying to rack up as many kills in a game as possible, I made a game of being the hardest moving target and to simply not die a lot.

You see, I looked at the game they were playing, which added pressure, turning the game into work, and decided to play the BattleTech game but not within the structure of the Masters system. Did I ever make Master? Nope. Did I occasionally annoy the crap out of the guys who took the game very seriously? Oh, for sure. *Oops.* Did I love playing and have a blast? I did, and that was my end goal.

DETERMINE YOUR WIN STATE

We have been told our whole lives there are rules. You get a job, work super hard, get promotions and more promotions. If you work really hard, someday you end up with that big paying job and retire. What about all the other things you might want to do, like write a book or travel the world? The Crunch Culture Game leaves no room for dream time or fun time.

When you join the Coast Guard, the "win state" of the game as an officer is making twenty years at least, but the gold standard is to become an admiral. The gameplay to get to that win state is to pick the right billets—what we call job assignments—with an operational career path seen as valuable by the service—specifically the promotion board—and make sure you have all the right bullet points for your officer evaluations. *Careful here, Player 1, there are some tricky spots when it comes to your boss liking you or not!*

I'll be real with you. I didn't give a flying fuck about making captain or admiral. I wanted to be an officer, sure. I wanted to serve in the Coast Guard, absolutely. But similar to playing in the Owens when the others were in the massive mechs, trying to rack up kills, I never had that "I had to make admiral goal or I was a failure" mentality.

By most metrics, my career has been a success, but guess what? I was passed over from the rank of lieutenant to lieutenant commander. That's right, I never made it to twenty years in the service; I never got to be what was considered a senior officer. By the metrics of the Coast Guard and many of my CG peers? I am a failure.

On the flip side, I left the Coast Guard with two master's degrees the service had paid for and a wealth of experience that made me a unique candidate. This helped me land a job faster and at a higher level than the majority of my peers who got out at the same rank or have gotten out since. (No joke, when I was going through the process to get out of the service, we were told we should be prepared to take pay cuts and not land a good job for up to two years after we got out.) So, while I didn't get the promotion I was told I should want, I have been successful in my career the way I wanted to be.

My game was about what I could do that challenged me or made a difference. This drive led me to be the first official blogger for not only the Coast Guard but the first flagship blogger for any armed service. It led me to take on launching the first mobile app for the Coast Guard. I became someone that senior officers knew would take a complicated or impossible challenge and run with it.

Now, I am not saying you shouldn't follow laws. On the contrary, a big part of metagaming is not breaking any of the legalities or hard rules of the game. In other words, don't cheat on your taxes, and don't decide that your metagame is to run around the office before your coworkers show up in your birthday suit, drink on the job, or otherwise violate HR policies.

Take a look around you right now. Think about the system you are in. Now, mentally take a step away from it and think about who you are and what you want to be when you grow up. Do those two things align, or are you doing what you have been told your whole life you need to do to be a "success?" Sticking to those win states you have been told are the end goal deeply restricts your ability to be creative, your ability to thrive. When you are playing a game you care about and believe in, it will shine through; you will shine and people notice that. People are drawn to passion, to that charisma you exude when you are doing "your thing" and are loving every minute of it.

METAGAMING AS A LEADER

Let's take this a step further and move away from the personal goals you set for success and look at it from a leadership perspective. Being able to metagame—set and define your success metrics—can help you build and lead a team, which is especially useful when you are working in a system with a chaotic leadership or a genuine lack of leadership.

If you are in a leadership position, you need to decide on goals for your team and how the players will be set in their roles as they work. If you keep your head wrapped around their role title, how senior they are, you are only seeing part of the picture and a part of their talent.

There will always be the system you need to play in, and that comes with some win states you simply cannot ignore. For example, making more money next year is a goal of any company, especially a publicly traded one. Ignore that and you likely won't keep your job long.

In my case, I couldn't just say "Naw, I don't think we are going to do more launches this year than last year" when I was the head of launch operations at AWS. What I could say was we were going to go ahead and do those launches in a new way that minimized burnout and had fewer errors. So while the system win state was more launches, my personal win state was keeping my people from burnout and building a system that didn't break.

When you are building your team, don't only look at the goals set for you; look at the team as a group of players who need to use their skills to beat the game itself together. Think about the game in a new and different way, outside of those metric goals you have set. Here are some tasks to get you started:

1. **Look at your goals and, without worrying about rank or title, list out the names of who you would put on each goal and why you chose them.** Not only why they would be good but why the project would be good for them. If a project isn't a good fit for a person—such as not enough of a challenge, something they have done

a bunch before and might be sick of, etc.—consider moving them to something to help them grow.

2. **Decide on the lead.** Look within those groups and decide, do you need an experienced leader for that task or can you give someone who hasn't had a chance to lead something before a go? If you decide to let someone new have a try at leading a project, make sure to set them up for success with a mentor.

Metagaming within a system can also help you set up goals and provide guidance for your people when chaos happens around you or if your leadership frankly has no clue what they are doing. Take a long look at the end state you want your team to have, what would the wins be for your team in the system you are struggling through? Make *that* the game you have your team playing, instead of trying to chase the endless shifting goalposts of a leadership org team that is as coordinated as a box of drunk hamsters.

THIS IS GONNA HURT

In 2024, the Oscars snubbed Greta Gerwig and Margo Robbie, failing to nominate either of them for the movie *Barbie* (2003.) In discussing the news with my friend and mentor Shannon Loftis (retired from Xbox as the VP of Game Studio,) she brought up in context of this chapter of the book.

"Greta won. She made a billion-dollar movie that moved the cultural needle and gave words to a generation, two probably of frustrated women, but [they] still snubbed her for an Oscar.

And while she shouldn't care, she likely feels it at some level. I do, and I didn't make the movie!"

Shannon brought up such a great point; this shit hurts. The world didn't end when I didn't get promoted in the Coast Guard but absolutely hurt because I had done a lot for the service. She asked me what I did to deal with that feeling, that pain, when I have faced it at points in my career. Honestly? I got angry that the system was set up in a lot of cases in a way that I was never going to be able to succeed.

So, fuck that. Fuck them. Break your own path. Take that dismissal and use it to fuel yourself. I am not saying I have always done this. I have cried, I have wanted to give up, but then I look at women like Shannon. She would humbly tell you she didn't move the needle. Retiring as a VP, Game Studios at Xbox, she was a glass ceiling breaker, an inspiration, and damn if she didn't say "Fuck it, watch this" to the naysayers.

Look for those people in your life or those you admire who have accomplished amazing things. They likely took the rules and made their own game of it even while they were taking the hits of being dismissed and put down. They were able to get away from the system they were told they were operating in to let their creativity and passions thrive. I bet a lot of them would admit they did it largely to prove the world—or some people in it—wrong.

Once you realize you aren't going to die if you don't follow the same processes as everyone else, and that you can set your own win goals, you will find you aren't tied down by the game anymore and can really stretch yourself and your abilities.

Remember, you can't game a system if you don't get in there to play in the first place.

CHAPTER 2

High School Bullshit

So you say you don't want to play the game, that you don't play games at all? I'm sorry to be the one to tell you this. It is all a game and you don't really get a choice if you are going to play or not. The only choice you get is who you are going to be in the game and how you are going to approach it. Dude, it sucks, but we have literally evolved this way.

A key part of understanding this is knowing there is no way to get away from one of the games within the whole system—the status game. You see, the workplace is not just a place where you "work;" it is also a social arena where status impacts how effective you are, if you get ahead, and heck, even your health—both physical and mental. It sucks, but the pursuit of social recognition, power, and influence within the social groups or organizational hierarchy is a part of being human.

The Status Game by author Will Storr is an outstanding book in this subject and goes into way more detail about the game than I will go into here.

—WILLIAM STORR, *The Status Game*[1]

Where you get to make your choice is within a social group. Two types of people exist: those who actively seek to elevate their status and those who prefer to maintain a low profile. Writing this book is the first time I have sought to elevate my status, if I am being honest about it, as it puts my name out there as I declare, *Look! I am an* expert *at this stuff!* Or at least I am good at telling random stories? Before this book, my work has been behind the curtain.

Hierarchy and organizational structures often play a significant role in defining the rules of the game, but you will find few places where these structures are more clearly defined than in the military. Between the structure of the service itself and the way members are "broken down and rebuilt" during the various entry points into the Coast Guard, from Academy to boot camp, you have a breeding ground for clique mentality and a coopetitive—cooperative but competitive at the same time—behavior.

The high school clique mentality exists everywhere; some people never seem to grow out of it. This clique mentality was incredibly prevalent in the officer corps of the Coast Guard, and man did it suck. Like in high school, there were groups within groups, and there were privileges afforded to some and denied others. I am not only talking about promotions—though you will find officers who came from the Academy are statistically more likely to get promotions—but little day-to-day things like getting the more choice watch rotation than someone else. It was like a nesting doll of douchery to deal with.

Here is the thing: in systems where conforming is the norm, where people feel they have to basically walk over each other to get ahead, standing out and being different, even worse being exceptional, will make you the outcast of these mean girl groups.

FLOATING HUNGER GAMES

While I was a junior officer (JO) on my first ship, I was the odd one out in the wardroom. I was told I talked too much, but when I was quiet, I was being weird or not engaging my peers enough. I wasn't into the party scene and so I didn't really drink when we all went out, which made me uptight. I was strict about following the rules, so I was, of course, a brownnoser. I spent extra time studying and working late, so of course I was a Goody Two-shoes. I was into nerdy stuff like tabletop games and sci-fi, and read way too much. My boss, seeing I would go above and beyond, did what many managers do—gave me more work because he knew I would get things done when he couldn't trust my peers to do so.

True story, he admitted this years later after we became friends that I was one he knew would get my work done with the least problems so he stacked stuff on me. "I could always rely on you" was his response and is the death knell of the mental health of so many of us overachievers and perfectionists.

What I came to realize the "problem" was? I didn't appear to give any fucks whatsoever about what any of them thought or about the JO Hunger Games of getting ahead. I was "weird." Did it actually hurt to be the one they talked shit about? The one treated like the outsider? The one that never got help, or always got shit on even in front of a command who did nothing about it? Sure did. A lot.

It made it even more difficult to navigate. The nicer I was, the more helpful, the worse it got. They always looked for ulterior motives that made sense to them; I was clearly trying to look good for the command.

Funny enough, when I went to our sister ship for a patrol while my ship was in drydock, I didn't have any of the problems I did in my wardroom. In fact, I made some of the closest friendships I would ever have in the Coast Guard. They became my good friends, and still are even almost twenty years later.

What was the difference between the two wardrooms? It could simply be the different personalities involved. It could also be that I went into the new wardroom wiser because of the pain of my first one. I did what we call in the neurodivergent world masking, making myself fit the mold that was expected of me. I imitated the patterns of my peers, speaking about only things they had first, carefully modulating how I spoke and who I talked to. The funny thing was, it was after masking that I discovered this was a completely different wardroom and they didn't mind that I was different; they embraced it.

Of course I played a part in the status game, knowingly or not, in my first wardroom. I made a lot of mistakes, compounded by the anxiety of trying to fit in. I hadn't planned to talk about this particular time in my life until the Coast Guard reached out to me almost twenty years after the fact with another unintentional lesson.

MAYBE I WASN'T CRAZY...

When I announced I was writing this book, I got the strangest message on LinkedIn. It was someone asking me if I had been on the CGC Jarvis with them. When I confirmed I had been on the ship at the time, he responded with:

"I remember you. You were OCS and I was a nav BM with [another crew member]... I remember you being incredibly bright and kind of being hated on because of it. That was my young junior enlisted perspective."

This was his perspective twenty years after the fact. I openly told him his message had made me cry—in a good way—and thanked him for reaching out. I let him know that tour was one of the worst times of my life, and to have someone reach out to me so many years later, to let me know I was seen... Not going to lie, that shook me to my core.

He went on to say:

"I truly believe the [Junior Officers] aboard were truly jealous and saw you as a threat. People were cruel there, and I hated it too. I just refused to believe the entire service was that way. Had a ton of bumps in the road, but it's up to me to be a part of a positive change."

If I had a potato for every time I have been told someone was hating on me or intimidated by me because I am bright, or scary smart, or some other variation of "oh my god, stop being smart, you are making other people uncomfortable," I am not sure what I would do with that many potatoes, to be honest; probably end world hunger, but the potatoes aren't the point.

There are two takeaways from this story that are important when it comes to how you play the game:

- If you are making your own path or are somehow different—be it neurodivergent, smart, or whatever it is—there will be people who hate on you for it.
- If you see someone struggling or being treated differently, reaching out to them can change their life… even twenty years later.

The status game can wreck you; utterly decimate you, especially when you are a woman who lives in a society that consistently tells you everything is your fault and that you did something wrong or are seeing the world wrong. Even if I was a weirdo, even if I was smart, or even if I was "competition" for my peers on that ship, the way I was treated was not okay. It was also all a part of a game I didn't know I had no choice but to play, and I didn't have the tools to deal with at the time.

There is no way the Coastie who reached out to me could have known how deeply his validation of that time in my life was going to affect me; that it would, after twenty years, make me feel seen in a way I didn't know I needed to feel seen. Yet there I was sitting in my office, sniffling and worrying about getting my shit under control.

In hindsight, of course, we can all see what this was—a part of the status game. Every JO is made to understand in no uncertain terms that while they are working as a team, they are actually in competition with every other JO around them for the next set of promotions. If someone else is doing something awesome, they might look better than you and you might lose a spot.

Another example of this is when I was in Officer Candidate School, I was debating if I wanted to take the flight school application test. I had always thought about it and figured, what was the big deal, just take the exam, right? Well, some of my peers, one in particular, started badgering me that I shouldn't sit for the exam if I wasn't sure if I wanted to go to the school; that I should only take the test if I absolutely knew I wanted to be a pilot because if I did well, I would be taking a spot from someone who really wanted it and dreamed about being a pilot. Stupidly, I didn't take the test and closed a possible door for myself.

Here is the thing: my taking the test wouldn't have impacted this guy, or the other men taking the test if I then decided I didn't want to go. What it would do, though, is show I had gotten a better score and possibly taken away a spot from someone who didn't score quite as well as I did if I decided

to go. I had been scoring higher than this guy and the others
on almost every test. I was a threat, and they figured out a
good button with me to get me to back out of an opportunity,
thus eliminating me as a potential threat. My self-doubting
ass fell for it.

Over time, what I have learned is that I always do the best
when I am being authentically myself. What I learned was by
trying to play down how smart I was—by staying quiet when
I knew an answer, or otherwise pretended to be something
I wasn't—made things worse. As my friend Corey Quinn,
the founder of the Duckbill Group, said to me:

"There are always going to be people who have it out for you
no matter what, so you might as well be yourself."

SURVIVING THE MEAN GIRLS

So how do you see the status game for what it is and navigate
it as best you can with minimal damage to your mental or
physical health?

- Don't get wrapped around the axel over status; focus on
  delivering high-quality shit. Sit down and list out your
  goals, both personally and in your current job. Those are
  your targets to deliver on.
- Authenticity, expertise, and competence are the way to
  succeed, even in the face of being the outcast or told you
  need to change who you are to be a part of the in crowd.
  Write down three to five things about yourself that you
  value and post them where you can see them regularly.
  The guiding light on what you aren't willing to change.

- Look for the others like you and forge genuine connections with them. Networking and supporting others can create a positive reputation that can help buoy you up when shit gets hard. Set a goal of attending one networking thing a quarter, or reaching out to different connections on LinkedIn to just check in once a month. Whatever is sustainable for you.
- Create a culture of collaboration and knowledge-sharing —i.e., does your company have an internal wiki? Does your team document their processes there? Helping others succeed will lead to reciprocal support, a healthier work environment, and generally make everything easier.
- Remember, at the end of the day, the only person you have to live with for the rest of your life is you. Don't do unethical shit to gain status or to be in the in crowd. Don't give up your integrity for the approval of others.

When you have accepted that you are a part of the game and realize status is always going to be a part of the game you have to play, it is important to look for the motivations and various types you are working with. Doing this is especially important when you are looking at the people who in some ways control your destiny—at least they might think they do—those pesky managers of course.

CHAPTER 3

Oh the Managers You'll Meet

Some data suggests that for almost 70 percent of people, their manager has an impact on their mental health equal to that of their partner and more than their therapist or their doctor.[1] That's a lot of power for one person to have over your well-being, and let's be real, it often sucks... a lot. For example, when I left a job where I had a "difficult" manager, to put it politely, my resting heartbeat went down an average of seventeen beats per minute. The thing is, there are times when we can't simply say fuck it and quit because our manager is difficult; we have to learn how to mitigate the damage they can do.

Most people know about military moves. Yep, we move every two to three years. In some branches, there are sometimes even shorter windows. This means you are regularly "starting over" with a new office, new team, heck, a new city in a different part of the country. This is another reason veterans are so adaptable to change.

Here is the thing: your manager's doing that whole moving-around-circus too, so you rarely make it through one billet with the same boss or even the same chain of command. So, to say that I have had my fair share of managers would be an understatement. AWS saw almost similar movement, where I had four managers in my four and a half years, not counting changes in skip levels.

Gartner, a provider of research and consulting services for businesses in the IT sector, declared in 2019 that there were four manager types: The Teacher, The Always On, The Cheerleader, and The Connector. They then go on to explain which type of manager has a more positive impact on their teams.

This is all well and good, but let's be real. Managers are often a royal pain in the ass even if they have good intentions. Sure, they talk about things like how an "Always On" manager can degrade team production.[2] Honestly, I found their approach to the manager types to be a little too sanitized and high-level. Not only that it is geared more towards what type of manager they say is the most effective which is great, but let's be real, it's surviving managers you don't connect with that is the hardest.

Throughout my career, I have discovered there are basically five types of managers, some easier to work with than others, but all workable except one specific type. As I am a Coastie, I, of course, had to give them nautical names. Of course, some personality types lean more toward one management style than another. For example, you won't find an asshole prone to yelling Orca. You also won't find an empathetic Blue Falcon.

THE SEAGULL

SPLATTERING SHIT SHOW

Seagull bosses can be awesome if you are a self-starter. They are the kind of boss that stays pretty much up high out of the way watching from a distance. What you have to look out for is that the problem with seagulls is that suddenly they will swoop in and shit all over everything, intentionally or not.

Similar to how there are many different birds under the name seagull, there can be various types of gulls as managers, and you will need to determine what kind of gull you have. Do you have the gull who is well-intentioned but overloaded so they don't mean to cause disruption? Or is it maybe a gull who has been thrown a bunch of new responsibilities they aren't as knowledgeable about so they are trying to stay out of the way but don't know enough to realize they are causing chaos?

I had one manager who never really spoke to us unless someone important was coming into town and then she suddenly was everywhere. This meant that until I figured out I needed to send her updates with a light level of detail on a regular cadence, she would swoop in and start claiming that things weren't being done. I also learned to double that cadence in advance of a visit from an admiral or elected official. This wasn't because we weren't effective, or were wrong; it was because she wanted to claim she had a hand in when she was asked about our projects by leadership. She wasn't a bad person; I liked her a great deal. Working for her was not difficult once I realized that she would be at the fifty-thousand-foot level until she decided to suddenly get involved in everything.

Managing up comes into play here. With a seagull, you have to be proactively sending them a lot of information so if they do decide to drop in on something, you can keep the spray of damage from the seagull crap to a minimum. I have found for most of them, a once-a-week email with details on the status of programs can be immensely helpful. Once you have figured out the care and feeding of your seagull, it's usually easy enough to work for them.

THE NARWHAL
AT LEAST YOU'RE PRETTY

Generally harmless, but equally useless, the Narwhal looks amazing on paper and leadership loves them, but they have no expertise to have gotten them to where they are. This manager talks an amazing game, they are charismatic as fuck, but when you scratch deeper than the surface, they don't really have any depth of knowledge or skill. While they are generally harmless, they can be endlessly frustrating because they make decisions on who is the most convincing on their team.

The trouble with the narwhal is that because they don't really know what they are doing, they can be very easy to sway and rarely take a solid stance on anything. This means that you can convince them that a course is a good idea one day, and by the next day, they have completely changed the plan because someone above them had a different opinion.

This type of leader happens quite a bit in the Coast Guard. For example, putting a captain who has absolutely no background in public affairs in charge of public affairs for the whole

Coast Guard. Why? It is a good resume bullet for them, even though they specialize in cutters or flying helicopters.

Don't get me started on the officers they put in charge of technology. There might be a handful of officers in the Coast Guard qualified to be the CTO (Chief Technology Officer) of the Coast Guard due to the lack of attention the service gives to tech as a whole.

In my experience, these managers are some of the most frustrating to work for due to their lack of taking a strong stance on anything and the way they are less qualified for their job than people who are on their team are. So the first step in dealing with a narwhal is to figure out the best way to convince them to listen to you. Getting them to listen is a delicate balance of showing your knowledge without making them feel threatened by making it clear you are going to use your skills to help them look amazing. Often, I call this telling someone to go to hell and having them not only think it was their idea but buy their own ticket.

The next step is to work with your teammates to provide a unified front; the more of you that support or agree with a plan, the more likely the narwhal is to latch on to it. You will need to tuck away your pride a bit, especially if you have more qualifications than your one-horned whale wonder.

The benefit of working for a narwhal is you can learn a lot from them on how to work a room and manage up. Narwhals are consummate politicians, and if you are anything like me—and hate politics—there is a lot they can teach you on how to work a system to your benefit.

THE OCTOPUS

KEEP YOUR TENTACLES OUT OF MY SHIT

Octopus managers are the ones that have their tentacles in everything, so basically the opposite of the Seagull. They stay close to the sea floor, are involved in everything their team is doing, and are rarely caught by surprise. This sounds horrifying, I know, but a good octopus doesn't get in the way as long as they are kept in the loop on everything going on.

Again, like the seagull, there can be many types of octopus. Unfortunately, a lot of times, a manager being an octopus stems from insecurity in themselves or a lack of trust in others, which manifests as an inability to let go or delegate. As you aren't your manager's therapist, you can't diagnose them, and I strongly recommend standing up in your next one on one and saying, "Yes! I got it, you are an insecure octopus!" At best, they will think you might be having some sort of medical event and ask if you need them to call someone for help.

One manager I had was involved in everything, to the point I felt like I wasn't actually in charge of my own programs at all. He was always in the mix to explain to me my job, to take over my meetings, and generally show everyone how on top of everything he was. It was incredibly hard to not take his management style personally, but with some guidance from a mentor, I realized that was just how this manager did everything and it wasn't about me.

So I started being proactive on briefing this manager and letting him know what kind of decisions I was leaning toward so he could have his say before we had a meeting or did something. This way, I kept him involved but was able to control the narrative a bit more while also giving him the chance to have his say.

What you need to look out for here is the octopus who also can't let go or delegate; this is where you get your pain-in-the-ass micromanagers. Similar to the seagull, you need to keep this critter fed, but they are likely going to want a lot more detail than the less aggressive octopus. This can be one of the hardest managers to work for, especially if they are an octopus with lower emotional intelligence who will come off as untrusting and abrasive.

Again, you will want to set up a regular cadence of updates for the octopus, but also will likely want to go a step further and sit down to discuss lanes with them on decision-making control, and get them to detail out when they want to be involved. This can take some skill, but what I have found often works is, instead of making it about territory, make it about how you want to help them optimize their time by supporting them. If this conversation happens in person, make sure to follow up with an email about what you agreed on.

THE ORCA
TIPPING SAILBOATS AND TAKING NAMES

The orca is the team player manager. This manager focuses on their people as a team first and will jump in to help with absolutely anything or everything. While they will delegate, they also make it a point to understand what their team is doing before getting out of the way. They pass along knowledge as they get it, making sure that skill sets are shared across the team so everyone can back everyone else up as needed.

The line between being an orca and an octopus is thin. The key difference is the level of trust you get from an orca is missing from an octopus.

Ariel Kelman (CMO at Salesforce) is one of the best examples of an orca manager I have ever had, though I am lucky enough to have had a few of them, including Admiral Joel Whitehead when I was stationed in New Orleans, and Maggie Carter in AWS Disaster Response. These leaders made it clear that we worked as a team, and no matter what your level, your input was valuable.

While writing this book, I talked to Ariel about his type of leadership style, and he pointed out it was just plain good business sense to listen to all the people in the room because everyone had a different perspective and a well-rounded conversation simply leads to better business decisions. He seemed surprised when I told him it was this method of leadership that made him stand out to me because far too often rank in a meeting outweighed potential knowledge for many of the managers I had worked for.

The only problem with orcas is they can often be system blind, meaning they don't pay as much attention to the politics outside of their team or the needs of other teams outside of their own. This can lead to issues in cross-team collaboration as the us versus them can sometimes get a bit competitive.

Orcas don't need much management, though I still recommend keeping them updated regularly so that when they are slammed, they are still getting information. Another big thing with orcas is you need to make sure they know what you "want to be when you grow up," so they know how to best utilize you both for the team and your career. Otherwise, in their enthusiasm, they might get you involved in a bunch of things that are not the best fit for your goals.

THE BLUE FALCON

RUN. RUN FAST. RUN FAR.

I can't take credit for naming this one, and you will notice this is the only nonnautical creature on the list. You know the military loves their acronyms. The Blue Falcon is used to describe someone who is a master of the art of team sabotage. It represents that one person who is willing to throw anyone under the bus, intentionally or otherwise. The term Blue Falcon comes from the term buddy fucker. Since buddy fucker was something impolite to say, the bird term was born.

The Blue Falcon finds a way to take the accolades for any wins while somehow making you feel like you are in the wrong for wanting credit for your work in the first place. So, in the corporate jungle, a Blue Falcon isn't a majestic bird; it's the manager who acts like they are a team player who totally cares about team culture and people, while in truth, they are only looking out for themselves.

Sadly, I have worked for a few of these. I had one manager who barred me from going to a meeting I had been attending weekly because she was my boss so they didn't need me there. Her issue was that everyone was used to being updated about my program from me. This meant she got less time in front of the command, so she decided to take over. I found out from other attendees she was taking credit for all of my work as though I didn't exist at all. She also misrepresented some ongoing cases to the point that eventually the admiral asked for me to return to the meetings because he knew he wasn't getting the whole picture after there were a couple of critical mistakes made.

In my civilian career, I have worked for a couple of these too. One manager would take my work and present it to leadership without my name attached to it at all, taking full credit. I found this out because, in an email from our leadership, they congratulated him on his outstanding idea. This same manager told me my experience as a veteran didn't count in "the real world." Another manager would talk all about a culture of work-life balance to the wider team but would never follow through with the promises for how we were going to improve. It was all performative.

If you realize you are working for a Blue Falcon, gird your loins and be prepared for a long-drawn-out passive-aggressive battle. The only way to combat a Blue Falcon is to document everything, making it harder for them to take credit or blame you if something goes wrong. If a conversation is had in a meeting that raises a red flag in your head, follow up with an email detailing out what was said in the meeting, even if it is under the guise of wanting to "make sure I got everything."

While there are ways to survive a Blue Falcon, it is the one type of manager you will genuinely struggle to grow or thrive under. The best you will get from this manager is examples of what you don't want to be when you grow up.

ADJUST YOUR TACTICS

The trick to dealing with these types is that you can learn to work with each of them as long as you see what you are working with. With every one of them, the key is learning the communication style that works best for the manager in question. Seagulls and octopuses need a lot of information to keep them out of your way, for example.

Now, I am sure you are sitting back thinking, *Well, she didn't mention the manager who yells at people or belittles them or the manager who says passive-aggressive or sexist things.* I am talking about manager styles, not assholes. You are going to find those anywhere you work, and certain types of managers can be not only one of the archetypes but an asshole on top of that.

For example, you can have a seagull who yells at their people, and they likely have a good reason in their head for why they are behaving the way they do. Let me say this in no uncertain terms. There is absolutely never a good reason or excuse for belittling someone, yelling at them, or saying something inappropriate.

Fuck all the way off with the phrase "assume best intent," which is the most recent iteration of "learn to take a joke" gaslighting.

The keys to working with any of these are:

- Learn to change your communication style to match the type you are working for.
- Give serious thought to your own style and personality and which of these types you can manage to work for and which types you simply can not.
- Remember that most people will not fit into a single type. For example, you can have a Seagull Blue Falcon. Those are the absolute worst, in my opinion.

You are likely going to need to ask a lot of questions to determine what kind of manager you have since many don't walk around with their tentacles hanging out. Luckily, I have some tips for how to get to the root of any issue. You just have to ask.

CHAPTER 4

Investigative Questioning

You remember that class where you were watching the clock, hoping the teacher might let you out a little early and then they asked, "Any questions?" and your whole body cringed because you knew there was that one student who was going to spend the rest of class asking any number of questions, most of them useless to you? What if I told you that studies have shown people who ask questions are actually more likeable?[1]

Learning to communicate with different managers and peers is key to your success in getting where you want to go. In some cases, it might make them like you more, especially if you are faced with a difficult manager, peer, or path. It, of course, depends on the questions you ask. One of the fastest ways to get on the right track is to learn how to ask the right questions and dig into what someone is actually asking for, not what they say they are asking for. This can be especially hard with managers like the seagull or the Blue Falcon.

Too often, people take what they are being asked for at surface value and do what they are told. Then, when it doesn't result in what the asker wanted, they deal with the fall out. At this point, you find yourself burning out and super frustrated for having wasted your time. Taking the time to examine who is asking the question or giving the task, as well as the situational landscape, and ask amplifying questions—questions where you get clarity on the ask and the reasons for it—is always worth it.

SEARCHING FOR ANSWERS

When you work in search and rescue in the Coast Guard, you have to go through SAR school in Yorktown, Virginia. The course is about four weeks long and teaches students from the Coast Guard, Navy, and Air Force how to perform search and rescue planning and operations in coastal and oceanic environments. After completing the course, you return to your unit, where you stand watch as a trainee with a qualified SAR Controller until you have enough time and experience to pass a qualification board.

Let me tell you, nothing teaches you to listen for what someone is or isn't saying as fast as taking calls for search and rescue. You quickly learn that what isn't being said is often more important.

Take this case, for example: a woman called in claiming her husband and his vessel was overdue. He was supposed to have taken his vessel out the day before and return, but he had not returned as of the time the woman was calling us. As I spoke with her, I noticed there were words she was using and a tone she was taking that did not indicate she was worried as much as she was mad. This tone, of course, does not mean that our team was not going to do the due diligence of investigating, but something about it set a flag in my mind that there might be something more going on; specifically, the level of anger in her words and phrases like "him not fucking telling me what is going on is just like him." Usually, even if a couple has had a fight, if one goes missing, the response is more fear than straight up anger.

While we were doing our due diligence, calling the marina and hailing his boat on the radio, we had another call with the wife. That's when someone asked her if she had tried calling her husband. I asked her if the phone was ringing or if it was going directly to voicemail. One would imply he just wasn't answering; the other would mean he was out of cellphone range or the phone was off. Her response? It was ringing at first, but on subsequent calls, it had gone straight to voicemail.

Something not many people know is that, in certain missing persons cases, the Coast Guard can get a warrant to check where the cellphone of a person was last "seen." We decided to get that warrant, because for all we knew, the boat had gone down or this person was in distress.

Well, the cell record came back that he was on the other coast—not in the ocean. Well, shit. Search and rescue is one thing; a husband who sold the boat and is on the other side of the country is not something SAR school prepares you for.

We called the woman back, and my boss gently broke the news to her that we had found his location and it was not a case we could go further on. Her response? "I knew it!"

You see, she wasn't asking us about an overdue vessel; she was asking us to find her husband, who had lied to her about where he was. To this day, I am convinced she knew something was up and never believed he took the boat out at all but called us to get the investigative work done.

DO YOU *REALLY* GET IT?

Call out and response is a common tactic in the military; one person calls out information and someone repeats it back to acknowledge they heard it. This is also a part of active listening, but to get to the core of what someone is really asking for, you need to not fall back on call and response; you need to repeat what they said and then expand. There will be other times when you will be asked a question as a leader that you simply do not want to answer.

Tell me what you want, (and I'll give you what you need).
—THE DOOBIE BROTHERS

First things first, don't play that game of telephone. Don't have someone asking you to do something someone else asked for that they heard from someone else. This creates information drift. By the time the ask gets to you, the information has been put through so many different filters and lenses it likely represents the original ask about as much as a modern-day chicken looks like its dinosaur ancestors. Go directly to the source.

After you have gotten to the source, take a moment to consider who is tasking you or asking something of you.

What is their experience? Do they know enough about the thing they are asking to even know what to ask for? Could there be some political motivation? Listen beyond the simple phrasing of what is being asked.

You need to really think about the way you or your team is engaging in a problem and not only look at what has been tasked.

- What is the core reason behind the task?
- What is the motivation of the person giving the task?
- What is the unspoken end goal?
- If someone said something you are doing is impossible, why is it supposedly impossible?

SO MANY PAGES

The Coast Guard webpage had been called by Gizmodo, in 2014, one of the most embarrassing government websites.[2]

"The red-headed stepchild of the armed forces has a hard enough time as it is, the least we could do is give them a website that doesn't look Carnival Cruise circa 1999."

Ouch.

I was in charge of revamping the uscg.mil site from six thousand plus hardcoded pages to a content management system. In other words, pages that had been coded by hand and never updated. This means there were pages that had HTML 1 from 1993 hanging around like ghosts in the attic. Imagine taking a copy of *War and Peace* and being asked to make it digital.

My job was to fix that. No big thing, right? Just take twenty plus years of web "design" done by hand and move it into a modern content management system and update the entire look and feel. The audit of the site and everything wrong with it was my capstone project in graduate school. For comparison, Amazon has an entire department of people for each of their various websites, including people whose entire job is to look at the user experience before the designers get to work. I had... well? Me.

When I was working on the scoping document—a ridiculously long paper on all the things that the page needed to be successful—I went through the process of getting feedback from the senior officers who were in charge. You have to understand, these officers did not work in tech, and they did not have a background in UX or UI. Many of them had made a career flying MH65 helicopters or cleaning up oil spills. I wish I had kept a recording of the asks they made, but suffice to say, it was all the shiny bells and whistles that went with webpages in 2014. Everything but animated GIFs.

At the core of all the shiny object asks were: we want our webpage to look good and not like a 1994 GeoCities cruise line webpage. Oh, and a site that doesn't take up quite so much server space.

For the record, they were nowhere near ready to broach the putting-things-in-the-cloud conversation, which they only started to delve into in 2023.

Here is where it became important to understand that, due to technical knowledge debt, they didn't know what to ask for beyond the appearance of the page. They didn't ask about search engine optimization, search on the page, user experience, or information architecture. All of these things go into the functionality and success of a webpage but weren't things that the senior officers were trained enough in to even know to ask questions about.

So, while they were asking for a good-looking webpage, the real ask was a sustainable page that could be run with limited backend knowledge by the majority of the people who were going to be expected to update it. A page that also didn't lose any data in the transfer from hard-coded HTML pages to a content management system, because of archiving laws when it comes to federal pages. A page that maintained the presence of the service online—easily searchable and with a modern UX.

In certain situations, we hear what's being asked of us, and we just want to follow orders. Okay, senior vice president (SVP) told us to do this, or SVP asked us to do that. So, at the end of the day, there's the question and then there's what you're going to answer with. And you don't have to give the expected answer. If you give the expected answer, you're actually restricting your ability to be creative, to be different, to be the one who comes up with a great solution.

You will often find people asking for what they think they want, not what they actually need to reach the end goal. Other times, you will hear someone asking for something that is impossible or a question that is going to put you into a difficult situation. In those cases, you can either reposition the question to get to where you are trying to go, or you can take the April 25th route.

THE APRIL 25TH ANSWER

My favorite example of a tactic to get around answering a question you don't want to answer is an example from the 2000 movie *Miss Congeniality*, starring Sandra Bullock. Without going into too much detail, it is a movie where the main character, an FBI agent, goes undercover in a beauty pageant to prevent it from being bombed. In one scene, William Shatner's character asks a contestant, Cheryl, who's portrayed as ditzy, to describe the perfect date. Cheryl talks about why April 25th is the best day to go on a date due to its generally pleasant weather.

This moment is portrayed for us to potentially laugh at her for being too dumb to understand what he was asking. But let's look at this in a completely different way. Instead, let's look at it as her answering the question literally. Now let's take it a step deeper and ask ourselves, was she actually wrong in the way she responded? Technically, she wasn't.

This method of answering a question in a way that it was not intended is one you can use to steer a conversation in a direction you prefer to get to the root of the question's purpose. With this method, you are intentionally using your knowledge of what is really being asked and channeling the situation in a direction of your own choosing.

You can save yourself a lot of time by responding to the need, not the ask. A warning goes along with this though: do not assume you know the base need without having asked more questions to dig into the situation. There will be times, like the woman looking for her husband, where you cannot ask the question you really want to, but in most situations, you can find ways to engage with your stakeholder or boss to ask those questions that really get to the core issue.

Here are some examples of questions:

- So if we were to do X-Y-Z, what result are you hoping to get out of it?
- What data brought us to this point? What are we looking for when we started looking at this particular data set?
- What have we already tried in this situation?
- Why was this system/program/process set up this way before?

These questions can help you get beyond the initial ask or tasking to the real end goal.

BUT IT'S ALWAYS BEEN DONE THIS WAY

Be wary any time you are working on a task and someone says you need to do something because that's the way it has always been done. Things have always been done a certain way for two reasons: either they are really the best way to do the thing, or no one has had the tenacity to stand up and go "This is stupid we should change it" and the follow through to change it. Check yourself when you say it.

When you are looking to find the core reason behind an ask, this issue often arises. You are being tasked to do something because the company has always done that thing. Take a moment and ask yourself, what is the goal of this task and is this really the way to get to that goal? If it can actually get you to the goal, ask yourself is it really the most efficient?

In a post-COVID-19 lockdown era, we are seeing a lot of questions about hosting and attending events. For decades, going to the big tech conferences and various industry conferences were something you did simply because it was how it was done. Now, many companies are asking themselves, did we really need to spend all that money sponsoring conferences? How much in sales did we really make from those events?

For example, CES (Consumer Electronics Show, one of the largest conferences of its kind in the world) reported the 2022 attendance was down 75 percent from the last in-person event in 2020. While numbers are slowly getting back to the pre-pandemic attendance numbers, they are nowhere near where they were before the global lockdown. Companies continued to turn a profit without hosting or attending conferences, in the short term, so now that the conferences are back, a lot of companies have simply decided to not attend anymore.

One of the best examples of companies deciding to opt out of how things have always been done is the Electronic Entertainment Expo 2023 (E3 2023.) This expo was known to be the place where big announcements in the video game industry happened, from hardware manufacturers to software developers to publishers. E3 was where new products and games were previewed.

The event was scheduled to take place June 13–16, 2023, but on March 30, the event was officially confirmed to be canceled due to lack of interest. Interest was lacking because multiple big-name studios, including Xbox Game

Studios, Sony Interactive Entertainment, and Nintendo, all announced they would not be attending E3 that year.

Instead of spending the money on the conference, a number of publishers made presentations of game announcements during that same time. Others used this break from the E3 timing cycle to set their own pace on game announcements and releases, thus breaking the "E3 is when these sorts of announcements always happen" cycle.

This question needs to be reframed. It isn't only what were we getting out of those conferences but what we hope to accomplish by returning to them now that lockdown is over. In my experience, there is also the issue that many companies tried to do virtual conferences and found them to be a resounding failure and are now conflating that failure with the idea that events aren't worth the time or money. I'd argue that there is a lot to be said for meeting people face to face and getting a chance to be hands on with products and projects.

So what are we losing by having less in-person conferences or attending less? While it might not show immediately in the money, it will eventually affect things downstream.

All of this is a prime example of not getting past the question of "Do we get sales out of this event?" Instead, reframe the question around events to what do they do that you were missing during lockdown, what do they do that another round of paid SEO can't do? When you reframe the question of what you get from events that you don't get from your day-to-day marketing tactics is human engagement.

Your company presence at the event puts people to the problem; it humanizes the logo and the product in a way that Zoom meetings or another set of stats on your Sunday NFL game hosted by AWS simply can't. Besides, let's be real, no one wanted to go to virtual conferences because we were sick of staring at our computers and would rather be honing the fine art of making sourdough by the time conference season came around during lockdown. Is your attendance at a conference beneficial to humanizing your company, to getting customer hands on the product before it is released?

When you understand how to ask the right question to get to the core of an issue, you will find that you have gotten to the next level of the game. You have broken that fourth wall and are now functioning at a level where you will be accomplishing those impossible tasks with an efficiency that will not only save you time but will help save your sanity.

Being driven to ask why is something that likely drove my mother crazy when I was a little girl. My drive to know more and insatiable desire to always be learning something new is part of what drove Ariel Kelmen to ask me to not only take on a leadership role at AWS as the head of launch operations but to years later head hunt me to take on a VP role at Oracle.

When speaking to one of my classes at the University of Washington, a student asked Ariel what he looks for when he is building a team. Ariel responded without missing a beat: intellectual curiosity. He proceeded to tell the class that what made me invaluable to him was I never assumed I knew the answer to what he was asking for, that while I had deep knowledge, I was always learning more and asking questions, and that I never said "That's good enough" but instead "How could we make this better?"

You need that curiosity to cultivate to ask as many questions as you can when you are doing your work. This curiosity needs to go beyond the what and into the why of the workings of the system you are operating in. Only when you have figured out why things are done a certain way and why something is being asked of you can you really figure out how to not only accomplish the face value ask but exceed the expectations of those around you.

Or you can look at it all and decide the issue is at the core and set to work fixing the real underlying problem instead of putting lipstick on a pig. It is highly likely that right now off the top of your head you can think of a handful of things that you would stop doing at work or dramatically change if you could, because they are not accomplishing the goal they are supposed to be.

I should warn you, this shit can be exhausting. In many situations, you will need to walk very carefully. There will be times when you will be told to shut up and do what you are told. There are times when someone won't want to share with you their true motive for asking for something. But there will never be a time when it isn't worth trying at least a little.

How to Look at the Ocean

The Mariana Trench is pretty much the earth's belly button, except it's so deep that any belly button lint was long ago compressed into crude oil. It's like Mother Nature's ultimate hiding spot for her lost keys, Atlantis, and all the socks that mysteriously vanish in the laundry. So yeah, that is probably what most people mean when they use the phrase "It's like trying to look at the whole ocean." In fact, according to UNESCO, only 5 percent of the ocean has been explored by humans.[1]

With this in mind, the phrase "trying to look at the whole ocean" makes a lot of sense when you tell someone they are attempting to do something impossible. The thing is, someone using that very phrase is what cued my brain to change how I looked at the launch operations I built at AWS—and how to run operations on a massive scale.

What if I told you the AWS launch operations program I built applies the same methodology the Coast Guard uses to bring ships into port? What if I told you I used that system to help launch more than eighteen hundred features of all sizes, regions, and net new products in my last year running launch operations alone?

"You do not rise to the level of your goals, you fall to the level of your systems."

—JAMES CLEAR, ATOMIC HABITS[2]

Sometimes, to find your path within a system, you need to learn how to connect things that might, on the outside, seem to have no connection at all. True creative problem-solving lives here and is what will set you apart from everyone else.

The idea that you have to have worked in a certain field because your experience from somewhere else doesn't translate is a whole basket full of horse manure. You see this a lot in tech, and especially in the game industry. That's a whole bunch of gatekeeping nonsense. The experiences running different programs and systems bring in a diversity of thought that can genuinely benefit your organization. I wish I could tell you how many times I have heard a variation of how veteran experience, specifically in the Coast Guard, doesn't translate to the "real world."

One day, not long after I joined a company where I was in charge of the launch marketing program, I was on a leadership team call to talk about our ongoing projects and upcoming plans. One of the things I had been headhunted by the CMO was to build a launch operations program akin to the program I had rebuilt and optimized for AWS. This process would create a tracking system for all the products the company was planning to launch, throughout all stages of the process from inception to launch, basically from the moment a team came up with a product idea and started building it to the day it was in the customers hands.

As I explained this on the call, one of my peers laughed and said what I was talking about was impossible and that, in fact, it was like "trying to look at the whole ocean."

Folks, never ever use an ocean metaphor on a third-generation Coastie, especially not in this situation because, surprise! We can in fact look at the whole ocean.

"Funny you should say that. Did you know we can look at the whole ocean in a sense?" I replied. "And the process to watch all the ships on the ocean and bring them into port is pretty much how we should run launch operations."

There was silence on the line. The leadership team moved on considering the matter closed, that the idea was impossible. This was another "Fuck it, watch this" moment to me. Yet again, my expertise was being dismissed and I was being told something I was planning to do was impossible.

To understand what I meant when I responded, there are a couple things I should explain how the whole ship-into-port thing works.

First, you need to know about the AIS system. The Automatic Identification System (AIS) is an automated, autonomous tracking system used in the maritime world for the exchange of navigational information between AIS-equipped terminals.

With AIS, both static and dynamic information about vessels can be electronically exchanged, which is done by receiving stations onboard ships, ashore in command centers like the one I worked on, or by satellite. Since 2004, the International Maritime Organization (IMO) requires certain vessels to carry an AIS transponder that both sends and receives data. You don't get to opt out of this, as it is a part of the Safety of Life At Sea (SOLAS,) though there are special circumstances for military vessels, obviously.

The AIS transponder gives you a heck of a lot of information. AIS transponders on boats include a GPS (Global Positioning System) receiver, which collects the subject vessel's position and movement. This information, along with other static information provided by the vessel's crew, is automatically broadcasted at regular intervals via a built-in VHF transmitter. This static information usually includes the flag of the ship—aka what country it is from—the port it came from, what port it is going to, a general idea of what the cargo is, and the number of people on board.

Then, with the use of special software, it can be processed and depicted on chart plotters or on computers. You can find a lot of examples of these sorts of charts online by looking up "AIS global data." What you see is limited compared to what I could see in a command center. Keep this in mind; it will be important later.

Even though AIS was originally developed by IMO as a standard to help vessels avoid running into each other and to help port authorities control marine traffic with more efficiency, it is used for a lot more today. Nowadays,

AIS information is used to facilitate the work of people in various occupations, such as port authorities and harbor masters, ship agents, researchers, first responders for search and rescue, vessel crews and their families, pilots, environmental protection agencies, recreational sailors, data scientists, etc.

Holy crap, that was a lot of shit you probably didn't ever expect to learn. How does this relate to product launches?

Well, think of the product, say a new software service, as the ship. Like a ship, that product has a captain. The lead project manager, a VP, someone who is in charge of making sure that product makes it to shore, and their crew, who is responsible for the ship having all its cargo ready to go. Similar to the static data a crew provides on AIS, the project lead should be able to tell you who is in charge, how many people are working on it, what the product is supposed to do, and the ETA for delivery; basically when the boat is expecting to be pulling into port.

The dynamic data then becomes that estimated arrival date, and it will need to be updated based on measurables from the project manager and team. Running into a bug? It's like running into a storm at sea, and you might push back your arrival time by a couple weeks.

So, to start your launch operations common operation picture—aka the tool you can use so everyone who needs visibility into what is going on has a "single source" of truth for in-the-moment data—you will need to have this data from each product group:

1. Team information
2. Product information
3. Estimated time of launch

The next part of applying the Coast Guard's method for port operations to create an efficient and dynamic operation is to build what we called a Quick Response Card (QRC) style process. No joke, I checked while I was writing this book and three years past leaving the role at AWS as the head of launch operations with at least one entire team change over; the process still hasn't broken. This is one of my personal success metrics: build a thing the people after you can't break but only improve upon. If you leave and it breaks, you failed.

Here is how to do that in some simple steps:

1. Create a list of all the gates your product must get through to make it into your customers' hands, from testing to security, to various marketing processes, you name it. All of it.
2. For each one of those gates, now write out the amount of time it takes for them to complete their work and mark anywhere a failure at that gate means an all stop—aka major bug means nothing else can be completed until it is fixed, and a new timeline needs to be arranged.
3. I recommend dividing these into a tier or type system because a net new product will need a lot more gates and be a heavier lift.
4. Hint: a ticketing system will *really* help with this. Stop making that face. You know I am right. I have used everything from JIRA to SalesForce, HoneyCode and

even Quip for tracking. The more customizable and automated your system is, the better.

Having things laid out this clearly will help your downstream teams rapidly adjust to changes as they happen. This minimizes wasted time—aka money—and keeps everyone working on moving forward uniformly. While it sounds easy, trust me, you are going to spend a lot of time figuring out steps one and three especially, because every product team believes they are special, and their product is different and needs to be handled in a totally different way than any one else's. Sorry to say, but that is very rarely the case, no matter what that SVP is telling you. Sliced bread has already been invented, my dude.

WATERFALL ISN'T BAD

So, what I explained above sounds a lot like waterfall style management, in time when Agile and Scrum has been all the rage. Yet, for this sort of operations management, this port style actually works. Hear me out.

Countries with a coast control the two hundred nautical miles of ocean, the water column, and seafloor as it extends out from their coasts. These are called a country's exclusive economic zone (EEZ). In this zone, the exploration and use of marine resources is a sovereign right to that country. The high seas refers to the ocean water column that lies beyond the boundaries of any one country, also known as areas beyond national jurisdiction (ABNJ).

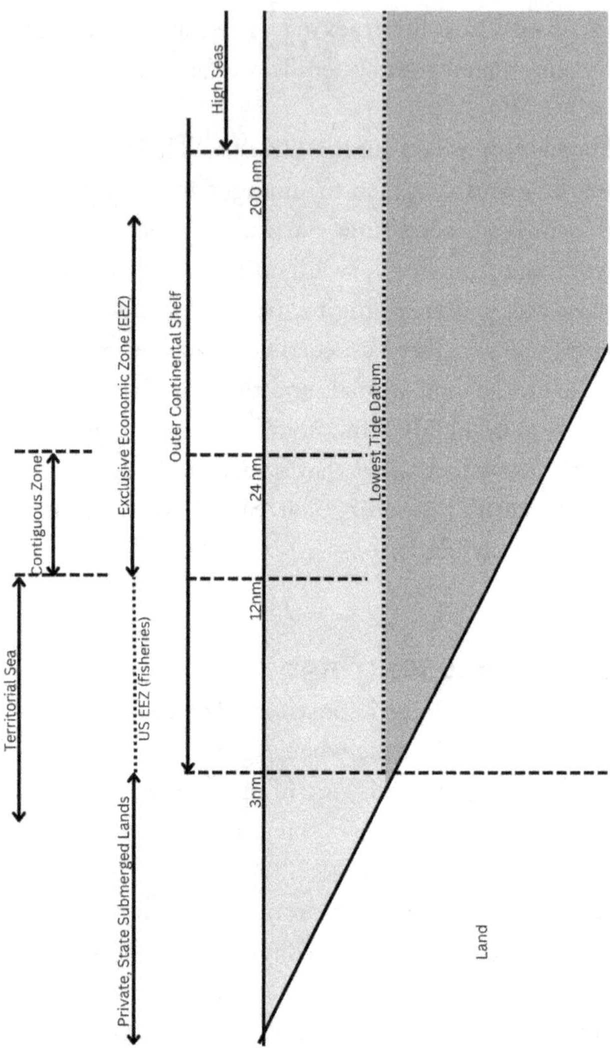

Turn the graphic sideways to get the ocean view, this isn't mountain climbing folks. Yeah, I know, this chart used to make my eyes bleed too. The important thing to remember is—closer to shore, more rules and more people you talk to.

This does not mean there are no rules on the high seas. It simply means there are less of them and they apply to everyone no matter what flag (country) the vessel is from. To be a bit flippant about it, it mostly boils down to: you must try to help save others, don't pollute, don't hit anything, don't throw anyone overboard, don't transport slaves, and don't mutiny. Thirty-seven articles are in the Convention on the High Seas, but for the sake of brevity, let's stick with those basics.

As you get closer to port, more rules will start to apply. First of all, you better let that country know you have entered their waters. Second, there could be rules against fishing, how you do it, and what species you catch. There can also be rules in certain areas that are protected marine environments. You also can't just go digging around on the sea floor in an EEZ. Like I said, a lot more rules.

When you hit twelve nautical miles from shore, you are now in the territorial waters of the country. Under international law, that area of the sea immediately next to the shores of a state is subject to the jurisdiction of that state. So that means a whole lot of rules and more check boxes the captain of the ship needs to check off as they head toward port. Basically, a vessel is bound by the laws of the country, but they have right of innocent passage. Put simply, passage not intended to fuck shit up.

Once you are within twelve nautical miles and heading for port, you will need to have checked in with your shipping agent, the port authority, a pilot if the port in question has requirements for one, as well as tugs and other agencies. You don't just get to haul in, parallel park your ship, and offload your shit.

SO HOW DOES THIS APPLY TO THE PRODUCT LAUNCH OR YOUR BUSINESS OPERATIONS?

Well, similar to bringing a ship into port, there are a lot of checks and balances your product needs to go through before you can put it up for sale. My experience is largely in tech, so I am going to talk about it in those terms. Speaking with a former leader at Xbox and now executive at Pokémon, as well as colleagues in the toy and beauty industries, product launches and operations are all similar at their core.

For example, in Europe, both Wizards of the Coast and Pokémon have to be hyperaware of the legal checks around lottery and gambling laws, due to the nature off the collectible card collection business, in that each pack has the chance of obtaining a card that is worth a not insignificant amount of money to collectors. So, whenever a new product line is coming out, they have to run through the checks to make sure they don't run afoul of those regulations. This takes a certain amount of time at a minimum that they need to account for in their product launch planning.

You also can't simply put a solution out into the cloud. It needs to go through user testing, a security check, and, oh wait, have you worked out what it will cost? When does it go from code name to real name? What about getting it on the webpage and sending emails? How's about did anyone check the name to make sure it isn't something that is going to make the internet laugh at you? (Looking at you, AWS

Snowball. Look it up on Urban Dictionary. Seriously. But not on your work computer.)

For each company, the groups involved in a product launch will likely be a bit different. Within a company, though, there will be a commonality of process once a product reaches a certain point. Each team will have their own service level agreement (SLA); in other words, the amount of time they need to accomplish their task in order to make the launch deadline. The blog team might need two weeks to get a post written and through approvals. The legal team might need three months to get all the documentation and regulations sorted for the new product. This would mean you should be getting the legal team involved sooner than the blog team.

So, similar to the checklists ships use for knowing when to call which team they need for mooring, you need to create a list of all the different teams involved with your product launches and their SLAs. This part is often the most painful part of the process because often teams have never been asked to document in this fashion and it can feel invasive. It also brings a transparency to operations that might uncover some inefficiencies. We will talk about how to handle those in a later chapter.

Remember, as Admiral Thad Allen (the 23rd Commmandant of the U.S. Coast Guard) was fond of saying, "Transparency breeds self-correcting behavior."

It's really going to suck trying to untangle the processes for a lot of teams, especially if this documentation has never been done. It will be worth it, trust me.

Once you have the documentation together, look over the SLAs and put them in order of how much time they take from the longest to the shortest. Now build backward. Use those old math skills, with X as the date of launch. What is the thing that can be done closest to launch? Social media? Cool, that's the last gate before launch is green to go. Keep going until you have worked yourself backward to the vessel being at the high seas part of the build, where they are out there coding their brains out with nary a concern about who is writing the blog post or how much the product will cost.

Many companies use what is called a Gantt chart for tracking this sort of thing, but those charts tend to be siloed into the product group itself or into one team tracking their own work. In my experience, it is rare there is a chart of this kind that covers every aspect of what is going in within the business. It tested using it for launch operations at scale, but Gannt quickly became unweildy and visually overwhelming. You need it to be as simple as possible, like a QRC.

It really is that easy. Create a checklist of things that must occur for the next thing to happen. A number of software systems exist that can help you do this in an automated way, but when you are looking at them, don't be distracted by the bells and whistles. Look for the simple answer.

WHOOPS, WE MISSED

Now, here is where the other pain point comes in. Missing gates.

When I was the head of launch operations for AWS, I used to brief CEO Andy Jassy every Wednesday on the status of launches throughout the company. Like many companies, we used a green, yellow, red model. Interestingly, we also used this model in the Coast Guard but usually to determine how dangerous an evolution was, but I digress. If something goes red or yellow and the launch date moves, often times, there is consternation from leadership. Thing is, ego aside, knowing about this sort of delay can save your company a lot of wasted time, and thus money, downstream.

By having a common operating picture where all the teams with downstream gates can see if something has been delayed, it allows them to adjust their workloads and priorities. This sort of transparency can also help clear communication lines and help diminish the risk of team infighting and discontent. Everyone has the awareness of what is coming and when.

Oh, but we have many secret projects, that we simply cannot tell those gossipy sales folks about, and heaven forbid we let the marketers in on our secret! First, I would say in my experience, your product team is just as likely to leak something as a marketing team. Fun fact, you can let teams know that something is coming and what type of thing—if is't a big brand-new service, for example—without giving away details that could cause damage online.

Building into your system a way to say the size of an incoming product, even if you can't give specifics, is no different than a ship saying it has three tons of cargo and the goods aboard are dry goods. While that doesn't tell me what's onboard, it gives me an idea of how much work will go into getting it in port and offloaded.

BUT HOW?

Now, as you are reading all this, it might be making sense, but you might also be scratching your head going, *Cool, but how the fuck do I do this sort of connection for other skill sets or seemingly unrelated things?* Trust me when I say it isn't just a trick someone neurospicy can do.

You can, in fact, train your brain to find connections by playing association games. Similar to theatre improv, these kinds of games make your brain form connections between seemingly totally unrelated things. It can be something as simple as playing word association games like Apples to Apples, or a game I will explain in Chapter 12 called Wikiball.

Those connections always exist if you look carefully enough for them and are using the right questions to get to the root of the issue you are trying to address. You can, in fact, look at the whole ocean if you know the tools to use, making almost any impossible task possible if you simply think a little differently.

CHAPTER 6

Dressing Drills

One night, on my very first ship, I was settling into my rack—that's what we call beds on a ship—after the first-night watch. I had just stuffed a sandwich in my face and was hoping I could fall asleep before the inevitable upset stomach set in. I was still getting seasick regularly at this point. The ship had the gentle hum that always came when we were running on the twin diesel engines many decks below where I settled in to try to get maybe five hours of sleep if I was lucky.

It was around midnight, and I was exhausted, having been on edge in that special way junior officers trying to get a qualification can be. Think of it like being under a microscope all the time, with everyone watching you and waiting for you to make a mistake. More on that anxiety later. For now, there I was exhausted, just changed into my pajamas, and I collapsed on the sleeping bag I slept in instead of the bed that was fully made under me. It was way easier to stuff a sleeping bag into a drawer in the morning than to try to make the bed, which was basically akin to trying to tuck your fingers into a toaster around a Pop-Tart. It hurt and never looked right after.

You know that moment when you are just drifting off, where you can still hear what is going around you, but everything has gone that gentle sort of fuzzy? Yeah, I skipped that entirely and went from awake one moment to completely out, like some sort of cartoon being hit in the face with a frying pan. This made snapping awake even more jarring. I had no idea what had woken me up, but I was wide awake out of my rack and throwing on my clothes by the time I heard a loud metallic clang. I didn't know in the moment that it had been an explosion; I just knew it was a sound I was not supposed to hear on a ship. Fully clothed in minutes, I had my protective gear in my hand and was running for the bridge as the alarm blared. Forget coffee. You want to wake someone up? That does it.

WHAT GOES BUMP IN THE NIGHT

"Now, there has been an explosion reported in the engine room" is not something you want to hear when you are out to sea on what was supposed to be a simple training cruise before your big trip underway to the Bering Sea.

Side note, if someone tells you, "Hey, you want to be stationed in Hawaii on a ship?" Say no. It means you are going to actually spend most of your time in Alaska seeing if you can pass a mushroom through your nose because you are so violently seasick in a category 3 storm—for reference Hurricane Katrina was a Cat 3—with sixty-foot seas for the majority of your tour.

When I arrived on the bridge after running through passageways filling with white smoke, I found out we had suffered a crank case explosion on one of our two engines. A crankcase is the bottom part of a marine diesel engine that houses the oil reservoir and crank mechanism that is connected to the pistons. Then pretty much everything else attaches to that case—transmission, gearbox, the engine control system etc.

So an explosion is bad, to put it lightly, especially because after the primary explosion, the shock wave has a breaking effect that reduces the size of oil droplets even more, producing more fuel for ignition. So you can get a secondary explosion causing a main engine room fire. And there can be shrapnel too, by the way. This is a vast simplification, but I am sure you get the point. Big boom.

Luckily, the situation was under control, no one had been injured, there was no major fire, and there was no hull damage. We weren't going to be roasted in a giant metal box. That helped bring the anxiety down quite a bit, but shocking no one, most of us didn't sleep a wink that night.

My boss came up onto the bridge minutes after I arrived, and I thought, "*Wow, the guy doesn't even have his boots on. Slacker.*" This story is about the *how* I got dressed so fast. Yes, you read that right.

GET THOSE PANTS ON!

Look, I am pretty sure the only folks who can get dressed faster than a Coastie on a ship are cheating spouses about to get caught. You see, when we are in boot camp or OCS, they make you get dressed fast. Really fast. Like less than two minutes fast from a dead sleep sometimes. Didn't do it fast enough? You are out in the passageway with your pants in your hands doing high-step running in place while a trainer who looks like they are preparing to eat your soul yells at you about how slow and incompetent you are.

Boots not laced? Enjoy some pushups. Pants not tucked into your boots the right way? Have some more pushups. Belt slightly off-kilter and not lined up with your zipper? You guessed it, more pushups.

Sounds pretty stupid, right? Trust me, when you are the one on the floor doing the pushups at 5:00 a.m. because you put your belt on backward, or even better, your roommate came out with only one boot, you are cursing how stupid this all is in your head. You are probably also cussing out the trainer and whoever spawned them from hell. You might even be cussing out your shipmate because, dammit, they always suck at getting both boots on.

The thing is, there is a reason they do it, and it's not to break you down and build you back up, which is what a lot of books about military training talk about. No, there is a specific reason to teach trainees in the Coast Guard to dress as fast as they can, especially when they are waking from a dead sleep. They do it so that when I was on my ship, out cold, and I felt the ship start to vibrate and was jolted awake, my muscle memory and training had me throwing my clothing on and getting ready to go, Go, GO!

Now, did my instructors explain that to me during training? Not right away. At the moment, we had to do it—in the middle of the night sometimes—because they said so, because that was how it was done. It wasn't until we were well into our training that one of the staff officers explained to me why they made us do the dressing drills, and that was only after I asked him point blank, as I was in the middle of doing push-ups for pulling a prank on another platoon.

After it was explained that "there might be times when we needed to be able to move fast or someone could die," I looked at the dressing drills a different way. They didn't seem so stupid anymore. While I can't say I didn't cuss my instructors out in my head during pushups anymore, I can say I understood why they pushed the issue so hard and was way less resentful.

METHOD TO THE MADNESS

At the end of the day, there was a reason for the insane things they were having us do, but what I took away from the entire thing wasn't just the lesson of how to snap awake and get dressed as rapidly as possible. The lesson here is two-fold. Training to get the muscle memory down is critical for when things get crazy, and explaining to people why you are having them do the crazy thing in the first place is also critical. I am not saying I would have been any less pissy at having pushups because my belt wasn't lined up right, but knowing the reason gave me the drive to do even better whatever the task assigned was.

Tell your people the *why* of something any time you can.

In my experience, there are a lot of times the communication around why we are doing something gets broken down in the urgency to get something done. As a situation's intensity heightens, communications have a tendency to break down if the existing system has a hierarchy that has not been designed with adaptation in mind.

A paper by Elizabeth Schrauben of Grand Valley State University supports this.[1] The paper talked about an E. Coli outbreak at Michigan State University and how as the situation grew worse, with more people getting sick, the problem was exacerbated by a lack of clear communication and response channels. The administration at the university did not want to go out with information before they had a clear source of the outbreak, meaning there was a void of information that was filled quickly with rumors.

The response got so chaotic when it was discovered that a nearby jail reported an outbreak they were blaming on turkey "... there was widespread anxiety on campus among persons who had recently consumed turkey and unease concerning the decision's merits among housing and food service staff..." The university in turn pulled all turkey from campus and residence halls, which was interesting because after school officials held a meet with staff, it turned out the turkey product that had caused the E. coli outbreak in the jail had never been stoked or served at MSU.

This sort of operational and communication breakdown inevitably leads to problems down the line. Problems like:

- Lack of documentation on a process to improve in the future

- Resentment from those you are leading, as they are fatigued by the chaos
- Failure to adapt and grow

Looking back on the dressing exercises and other oddities they taught me in bootcamp, I can tell you things will go easier for you if you are transparent in your motive for asking for something. This becomes even more true when you are asking for something that might seem silly to others, something difficult, or something that has never been done before.

When I was at AWS, in the lead-up to AWS re:Invent or any of the summits that had product launches, I would insist on having a practice call. No, not a meeting about a meeting, which I am completely against. This was literally roleplaying the event call. Commonly called a tabletop exercise in the military, it was play-acting the event as though it was happening without actually, you know, launching the boats or in this case the webpages, cost calculator, new product, or whatever else.

I made it clear to those who would be participating in the event that this was not an optional call, that I expected everyone to be on the call and engaged. The purpose of that call was to run through the "sheet," as we called it. This sheet had the operational plan for the event, what time it would start, and the times for every significant movement throughout the launch event.

This meant the leader from my team running the call would be calling out "Webpage, you are clear to launch," and the web team was expected to respond "webpage launching." Then, as soon as they were done with their task, they would loudly call out "Webpages launched, ready for QA," and my launch leader would respond "QA leads you QA your pages."

Each call and response was specific to the task being done, and if there was a call and no response, that indicated a breakdown or a problem. If there was a problem, the team with the problem would call it out clearly. "Launch lead web batch two is NOT live." And a member of my team would have a sidebar with the team in trouble either on the call or, if we were in person, at the computer of the team with the issue.

Did anyone have a clue what I was trying to do when I first set things up this way? Absolutely not. Did people mock it and think I was being "all military?" They absolutely did. So, as I was teaching them how the calls would be run, I explained to them why I was doing it.

When launch operations at a company like AWS are happening in real-time as a part of a show, things have to run seamlessly. In the past, people would run into a problem and it would cause cascading failures because they got so focused on the problem they forgot to tell any of the other moving pieces something had gone wrong. When many of these pieces were reliant on the segment before going smoothly, you can imagine how fast this snowballed.

By clearly announcing the stage we were at to the entire room, or over the call, the launch leader was making sure everyone in the room was on the same page. The response call from the team on deck had two purposes. One, it helped the launch lead know that the team knew it was their turn and wasn't distracted, and two, it let the room know that the next step had begun.

The call and response was not the only time I used the train the response memory of a team trick the Coast Guard taught me, and it is one I strongly encourage you to use with your teams. Shows have rehearsals for a reason, and you should too.

Once I explained why the process was necessary, I needed to also explain why the rehearsal call was necessary because I didn't want the first time they heard the call and response to be in the moment. I wanted them to have done it before, to know what it felt like. We even threw in some errors so we could run through how it would work if something broke. Teams grew to love being the one that "broke" during a prep call, getting into the role and making up insane, often hilarious failures to call out.

Did I need to explain all of this to people, and keep explaining it with each new event? I absolutely did. I also needed to explain how call and response worked every time. Thinking, *Oh everyone on the call knows how it works, the new people will catch on* is dangerous. First, because the people on the call don't live in my head and do the work I do every day, it might have been a year since they last did a launch. I don't know how much they have forgotten. Second, because of information drift.

Information drift, in this case, is my way of saying you are playing a game of telephone. Sure, someone who did a launch with you three months ago explained to the new person how these calls work, but they are telling it through the lens of their experience and their memory. Small details get changed this time, and those details get changed a little more as the new person then tells someone else. This information drift can be a beast to wrestle back, so it is better to reset expectations and understanding at the beginning, every time. Never rely on communal knowledge.

You can tell people what to do, and if you are in a position of power, they will likely do it, or you can tell them what you are doing together and let them in on why it is important, and they will be in it with you.

Were there still people who thought it was stupid and didn't want to "play act" a call? Of course there were, but you will find the majority of people want to be a part of the action. They want to do a good job, and they want to be a part of a team, and by being open and letting them be "in the know," you are making them a stakeholder in your efforts.

Move away from having people do what you tell them to because you said so, even when you think you don't have time or shouldn't need to explain why something is being done. By being clear and transparent on why you are asking for something out of the norm, you are setting the pieces up to be collaborative in a new way—a more team-oriented way.

When you are trying to teach people a lesson that isn't entirely obvious—and never assume it is obvious—it is in your best interest to explain what you are trying to teach and why. Even when time is of the essence, this type of transparent leadership can be critical to your success in stressful situations. It also has the secondary effect of forcing you to be able to articulate your why.

If you can't explain to people why you are having them do something, should you even be having them do the thing in the first place? The answer is likely no. It is worth spending the time on the front end to explain what is going on rather than to burn it on the back end dealing with problems.

So get to doing your own dressing drills.

1. Describe what needs to be done to the team. It might be a big event, a product launch, etc.
2. Set up a time that you will go through the exercise without distractions, with time immediately afterward for review.
3. Run the exercise like it were the real thing. Don't let people half ass it.
4. Take copious notes on what goes well and what doesn't.
5. Review immediately upon completion what worked and what didn't.
6. Follow up with everyone on how it went in writing, including any changes you will be making moving forward.
7. Don't be afraid to rinse and repeat this until you feel comfortable that everyone is on the same page.

Sure, some people might think this is weird, but I have yet to find someone that didn't see the value of prepping in this style when an event goes off flawlessly—even in the face of things like Amazon Prime Day crashing your system an hour before an event. Just saying. Sometimes people will think you are being weird, whine that you are wasting their time, or underestimate you and what you are doing. Thrive on that shit, and if you're not sure how, it's a good time to head into the next chapter.

CHAPTER 7

Embrace the Underestimation

Learn to let people underestimate you and then prove them wrong. It is not worth your time to try to argue with someone who has already decided you can't do something—because it is impossible or because they think *you* can't do it, doesn't matter which—or because they have decided you are whatever they have made up about you in their mind. Their preconceived notions of you have literally no bearing on reality.

"You know, I look like a woman, but I think like a man. And in this world of business, that has helped me a lot. Because by the time they think that I don't know what's goin' on, I then got the money, and gone."

—DOLLY PARTON[1]

Nothing is quite as viscerally satisfying as proving people who said you couldn't do something, that you were less than, wrong. The going back to the class reunion and showing all the bullies they didn't have a clue what they were talking about, living better than your ex, all of those things are common universal feelings. We make so many movies and shows about that underdog getting a moment of victory for a reason.

So instead of being insulted when someone underestimates you in the professional setting, take the time to remind yourself that their underestimation says more about them than it does about you and then go about showing them and everyone else that they were talking out their ass.

Probably my favorite pop culture example of the underestimated taking the prize is Elle Woods. If you have not seen the movie *Legally Blonde*, I strongly recommend giving it a watch. To be entirely honest, while the movie is over twenty years old, she remains the pop culture icon of underestimated women everywhere.

Obsessed with pink, a sorority girl with perfectly blonde hair and a bubbly personality, Elle is consistently underestimated by almost everyone in her life, from her ex-boyfriend to other Harvard students, to her professors. Over the course of the movie and many amazing pithy quotes, Elle proves that she is brilliant and a legal powerhouse in the making. She even goes so far as to win the court case she is interning on for a client that her #metoo level gross professor was half assing his legal defense of.

While the outside world might have seen Elle as a walking fashion magazine, she quickly proved she was no damsel in distress, that she was fierce and driven. She ends up as the valedictorian of her class, giving the triumphant class speech at graduation. In some ways, Elle underestimated herself, in that she originally decided to go to law school to try to win her ex back, and ended up finding her own strength and going further than the Elle at the beginning of the movie even dreamed.

We love an underdog. It shows up time and time again in movies, in the news, and across the stories we read. Underdogs are always underestimated, and that is part of what makes their story so satisfying—and probably why there is a *Legally Blonde 3* movie in the works! So instead of getting pissed off when someone underestimates you, embrace the fact that they just gave you a movie arc that will leave them in the dust and looking a bit silly. Seriously, look at the ex in *Legally Blonde*; he is the ultimate joke punchline.

Women and BIPOC are of course not the only ones underestimated. Men run into it as well, especially men of color or men who don't have the "traditional" education or resume for a space. As a manager, I dealt with this when one man on my team was demonstrating his educational bias against one of his team members who hadn't gone to college. This team member, a young gay man, had not gone to college but had gone straight into the workforce and had worked his way up. His story was inspirational to me, if I am being entirely honest.

Let's call him Dylan. Dylan had started at AWS working in the restaurant that was in the basement where employees would go to eat. He had experience as a chef, which got him the job, but his drive and ability to organize soon had him help manage the little eatery. Soon, AWS employees noticed

Dylan was amazing at his job, friendly, and organized. He was encouraged to apply for an administrative assistant job for one of the executives in the building, and just like that, he got the job.

That was how I met him. He was helping manage a calendar for an exec I supported and soon was helping us with projects. I appreciated how proactive and take charge he was; he had a hunger and a drive to learn more every day. So when I had head count open to join our team as a junior program manager, we brought him aboard.

The issues arose when I got promoted, and my team structure changed and Dylan was placed under one of my directs. Even though he was still on my team, he now had a new manager, who, on more than one occasion, mentioned Dylan's lack of college education. I had to counsel that manager multiple times that just because he hadn't gone to college, Dylan had worked his way up, had outstanding organizational skills, and knew the ins and outs of AWS in a way his new manager did not yet. I also had to remind the manager that yes, due to not having gone to college, Dylan might not do things the way that the manager or I would with a traditional background, but that didn't mean he wasn't valuable to the team.

Dylan continued to show his value, proving the underestimation wrong over and over, but unfortunately, the relationship with the new manager never improved, and not long after I moved to another role at AWS, Dylan left the company. Don't worry though he is doing great.

I will say this: if there were ever the chance again, I would hire Dylan in a heartbeat. He taught me a lot. Sadly, the truth of the matter is that, for some people, no matter how often you prove them wrong, their internal bias against you will not go away and that is frankly on them. Fuck 'em.

Another underestimation situation moment in the reverse, that happens once in a great while, is when someone tells you, without any prompting, "Wow... I underestimated you." And if the universe is feeling really sparkly, they even say, "I'm sorry."

I was standing in my office— real office, with a real door—at just twenty-six, something I didn't realize was odd until I joined the corporate world. This development was very exciting for me after spending my first two years in the Coast Guard on a ship where my office was also my bedroom that I shared with two to three other women at any given time. The job itself was my dream job. I was running the public affairs for an entire district, one of the largest in the Coast Guard, even.

So there I stood, uniform spiffy, listening to the sounds of my team getting ready to head home for the day, when I heard a gruff voice I had learned to dread a little. "Can I come in?" Sure, it was a question, but when the voice of the surly Command Master Chief was heard, you kind of did what he said. This guy had given me a hard time since I joined the unit almost a year earlier. To be honest, on more than one occasion, after a meeting with him, I had retreated to my office to get my shit together so no one saw I was about to cry.

Squaring my shoulders and mentally adding a cocktail to my evening plans, I welcomed the master chief into my office. He came in and shut the door. Crap. Crap on toast, I was in trouble. Nothing good ever came from a visit from the CMC.

He took a seat in the chair across from my desk and said words that to this day I never could have expected.

"I owe you an apology."

I sat in my chair because, to be real, my knees kind of buckled. There was this momentary short circuit in my brain like I hadn't heard him right. I probably looked like I was high or something as I slow blinked at him and asked him, "For what?"

He went on to explain he had made some assumptions about me when I first was assigned to the unit. He thought I had gotten my job because of who my dad was, and that I was going to roll in and think I was special and could get away with anything if I batted my big blue eyes because the admiral and my dad knew each other. He said he wanted to apologize because he had made assumptions and underestimated me and now knew that I was not only smart but really good at my job, and he appreciated that and appreciated working with me.

Without waiting for a response, he got his grumpy ass right back up and strolled out of my office like he hadn't just dropped a bombshell on me. Getting yelled at, sure, but an apology for underestimating me?

So yes, both women and men are underestimated, but statistically, being underestimated and undervalued is a problem that women and people of color face more often. In a paper published by MIT titled "'Potential' and the Gender Promotion Gap," researchers found that women received higher *performance* ratings than male employees, but received 8.[3] percent lower ratings for *potential* than men. The result of this was that female employees on average were 14percent less likely to be promoted than their male colleagues.

To figure out whether women and men were assessed the same in terms, the researchers studied data on thirty thousand management-track employees at a large North American retail chain from February 2009 and October 2015. While women made up about 56 percent of entry-level workers at the company, the number dropped as the rank level got higher; 48 percent of department managers, 35 percent of store managers, and 14 percent of district managers.

The company used the Nine Box rating system, which is a numerical talent assessment tool that compares performance and potential using a three-by-three square grid and a low, medium, and high scale. While this might sound all scientific, having been through the system a few times as a manager, I can tell you they are completely objective.

The researchers checked the Nine Box data for comparing male and female employees and were able to show that "potential ratings strongly predict promotions." An employee moving from medium to high *potential* in a Nine Box assessment corresponded to a 75 percent increase in the likelihood of promotion. There was only 27 percent increase in the likelihood of promotion when moving from a medium to high *performance* rating. This means that the objective system where the manager estimates your potential is given more weight than the subjective system of performance metrics.

Before you think this underestimation is only in business, it has also been shown to appear in academic situations in the differences between male and female PhD candidates. Two studies with experimental and qualitative data provide converging evidence in support of this assertion, showing that overqualified women were seen as more committed to their careers than qualified women.[2]

This happened because overqualification helped overcome negative assumptions about women's career commitment. Evidence revealed that hiring managers rationalized women's overqualification in a way they could not for men by relying on gender stereotypes about communality, as well as making assumptions about candidates' experiences with gender discrimination in previous jobs. This study basically shows how women have to overcome underestimation of their abilities by being overqualified for a position in order to get a shot.

SUCK UP YOUR PRIDE FOR THE LONG GAME

So how do you do this? is usually the question I get when I am asked about how much I enjoy being underestimated. This usually means one of two things: how do I just *let* people underestimate me, or how do I *get* people to underestimate me? It wasn't until a friend pointed out to me that I didn't just let a guy I was playing a board game against underestimate me, I encouraged him to do so. She wasn't wrong.

How do you just let someone underestimate you? The natural inclination when faced with some judgmental sack of three-week-old sandwiches prejudging you is to get angry, to vehemently protest this injustice. The inclination to respond immediately and dare I say aggressively to this sort of thing is more common in Western cultures.

Here is the thing: their underestimating you is about them. Not you. Their underestimating you is their prejudices, their lack of intellectual curiosity, and whatever other bullshit is in their head. All of it is them projected on you. So, in your head, think of their nonsense being directed at you as something they could easily be directing to the wall behind you, for all they know about it.

Use that mental model of "They are talking to an imaginary animation of you in their minds," and find a little spite in you somewhere. Not the "change out their lactose-free creamer for whole milk right before a four-hour meeting" kind of spite, but spite that gives you that little inner voice of *I am going to prove them wrong. I am going to prove them so wrong they will come right back around to being wrong all over again.*

Then it is no longer about them underestimating *you*; it is about them not reading the room, not having a clue what is really going on. That makes it so much more fun when you do what they said was impossible, when you are more successful than they ever thought you could be.

How do I *get* people to underestimate me?

This question is the other one that comes up a lot. So, I never advocate for PSYOPS at the office, or lying about who you are to get someone to think you are something you are not. What my friend was talking about is how, not only did I not correct someone for underestimating me but she claims I lean into or emphasize whatever I think is causing them to underestimate me.

Also, I know that because I have a "young" face, according to my mom—a round Cabbage Patch Kid knock off, if you ask me—some people are going to think I am too young. Others will underestimate me because I am a woman, or because I often have ridiculous color hair and tattoos—tattoos that I dare show when giving keynotes.

People tend to look at me and brush me off or count me out for a lot of reasons. I see no need to correct them of their assumptions. In fact, I find them entertaining. Sometimes I feel like I am keeping them in the dark about some joke, like how everyone around them knows they have toilet paper on their shoe and a kick me sign on their back, but no one is about to tell them.

"I'm not going to limit myself just because people won't accept the fact that I can do something else."

—DOLLY PARTON[3]

In an interview with Chief (the Executive Women's Network), I said sometimes I know people are assuming that it's because I'm a veteran that I am so organized and strict or am being a hard ass about something.[4] If they are busy assuming it's because I am a vet, they are less likely to go with the gendered observation of me being an assertive bitch. I am fine with that. It took a while to learn to be fine with it.

So, if someone's underestimating my work or me and I can use it to my advantage, I am going to make something of that. It's not like I am going to talk them out of it only using my words; simply a word of warning. Sometimes proving that person wrong doesn't happen fast. Hell, you might not be able to prove them wrong during the time you work with them. Just let that little spite fairy who hangs out on your shoulder with a running list of names of people who told you something couldn't be done keep you going.

EMBRACE BEING THE UNDERDOG

In movies and in video games, nothing plays to the audience quite the way the underdog beating the odds does. This is your game. Be that underdog everyone loves to see success. Those characters are always the hero of the movie.

Think of it as doing Aikido instead of Krav Maga, you are just using your opponent's weight and momentum against them. Instead of blocking and punching and creating a concussive force, you flow with it and redirect it to your benefit.

This will mean sucking up your pride quite a bit, which can be incredibly difficult. I have had situations where I had someone explain to me how a program I built worked, and explained it wrong. Instead of interrupting them as they talked in a room full of people who also knew I had built the program and had two master's degrees that applied to the situation as well, after he was done speaking, I simply smiled and told him it was always interesting to see how someone described one of my programs a few years after I had built it because it let me know how to build it better in the future so there were no misunderstandings.

I watched as a few of my coworkers did their best to not start laughing and the man as he tried to figure out if I was being rude or not. I had pointed out that I needed to build the program better next time, so he had helped me? But wait, I had also said so there were no misunderstandings, so was I saying that he had not been right? It was a careful balance to strike, and if I am being totally honest, I have no idea how I managed to do it in that moment other than listening carefully and responding with intention.

Remember:

1. People's judgment of you, their underestimation, says more about them than it does about you.
2. Don't argue with them. Declaring your value will not change their mind.
3. Make a plan on how you are going to over deliver on whatever they think you can't do. Get into Harvard like Elle Woods, so to speak.

The other fun thing about being underestimated is when people think you don't understand something, it gives you a lot of room to play by your own rules, to be a maverick in sometimes well-established systems. Then you can innocently blink your eyes and say, "Oh, really? No one has ever done that before?" when you succeed. The trick is to know how to avoid falling to people's low expectations or being a dipshit.

CHAPTER 8

Be a Maverick...
Not a Dipshit

I have talked a lot about metagaming and learning the rules of the system you are in so you can find ways to beat that system. Now, I hate to tell you, but I am about to put some constraints on that shit.

To be a "maverick"—what an overused silly word that brings to mind Tom Cruise in aviators—you need to understand the rules enough to *innovate* on them, not break them. You need to understand the difference between rules and laws. I don't only mean the laws the government enforces, though I mean those too, but the constraints around engagements and operations there for unchangeable reasons, like physics, for example. You can't just say "Fuck physics" and do whatever you want. Some laws literally can't be broken, and trying to do so will likely get someone killed.

At the time I am writing this book—the summer of 2023—a news story is dominating the internet from social media to news sites. The story is so dramatic that my team asked me about it, and various others through my day-to-day have wanted to talk about it. It captured the attention of the entire world for weeks. Hell, my dentist asked me about it.

The OceanGate Titan sub incident.[1] If you ask any submariner from the military, you will hear all sorts of interesting phrases they have for the CEO of the company and the corners he cut in building his "sub." Dipshit is the one I have heard the most often. I spent a lot of time talking to my dad about this case, because as a naval architect and marine engineer he is my ultimate cheat code to understanding any type of ship building.

If you managed to miss this incident, here is what happened: a billionaire thought he knew better than more than a hundred year's worth of shipbuilding and built a "submarine" to take tourists down to the site of the Titanic. The Titan submersible was a twenty-two-foot-long vessel operated by Everett, Washington-based OceanGate Expeditions. It first made a voyage dive to 13,100 feet in December of 2018, according to the company's website, and first dove to the site of the Titanic—about 9,186 feet beneath the Atlantic—in 2021. They planned for it to make eighteen such dives in 2023.

The $250,000 per person expedition was promoted on the now archived version of the OceanGate website as "a chance to step outside of everyday life and discover something truly extraordinary." As of the writing of this book, the OceanGate site simply declares they have shut down all operations. Here is how it went down:

Sunday, June 19, 2023

Heading to the site of the Titanic wreck, roughly 900 miles off the coast of Cape Cod, Massachusetts, the sub started its descent of 12,500 feet below sea level.

It was 9:00 a.m. Atlantic Daylight Time, according to Miawpukek Maritime Horizon Services, which co-owns the Polar Prince, the mothership from which the Titan deployed. At 11:47 a.m., the twenty-one-foot submersible lost contact. So basically, communications between the sub and the surface vessel were lost one hour and forty-five minutes after descent had started.

At 6:10 p.m., the submersible failed to resurface as scheduled. Authorities were notified at 6:35 p.m., launching an international search and rescue effort. Now, why they didn't call for help earlier, as soon as they lost contact, is something I have a feeling will be coming out in court cases that will likely go on long after this book is published. Let me just say, as someone who has done a fair bit of search and rescue, I find the timeline it took them to call to be concerning.

Monday, June 19 – Thursday, June 22

The sub's ninety-six-hour emergency air supply meant Thursday morning was a crucial search target. That was when the men would run out of air. US and Canadian coast guard crews scoured the ocean's surface and used sonar to listen for sounds far below the water. Commercial ships also assisted in the search, as is standard with these sorts of incidents. See the chapter on helping people out because it is the right thing to do, where I talk about the safety of life at sea.

In a statement Monday night, OceanGate Expeditions said it was taking "every step possible" to return the five crew members. On Facebook, an expedition participant on board the Polar Prince at the time urged people to "Think positive. We are."

Tuesday, June 20

Sonar picked up banging sounds from underneath the water in the North Atlantic Ocean while searching, according to an internal US government memo on the search, which gave many people a burst of hope. The reality is the ocean is actually a fairly noisy place and those sounds were, in the end, not that of the submarine. Tuesday afternoon, US Coast Guard Capt. Jamie Frederick estimated the vessel was down to forty hours of oxygen. Officials were unsure whether that was enough time to rescue those onboard.

Responders established a unified command to handle the search. The US Coast Guard confirmed the detection of underwater noises. The search area had increased to "two times the size of Connecticut."

Then, the last day of the search, two ROVs were deployed as part of the search effort. The Coast Guard released the news that a debris field had been found by the ROVs. It was the Titan.

Let's just say, with what happened to that vessel, there are literally no bodies to recover, just organic material.

SO WHY AM I BRINGING THIS UP IN SO MUCH DETAIL?

This extensive search, and devastated families, were all because one man thought he was smarter than hundreds of marine engineers and could throw the laws of physics to the wind. They say don't speak ill of the dead. Well, in this case, it is hard when the man responsible for the failures is CEO Stockton Rush, who was in the vessel when it imploded. Now, whether he and his company are legally responsible is yet to be seen, but here is the thing: he was warned multiple times by a number of experts why his design was unsafe.

"In your race to [the] Titanic, you are mirroring that famous catch cry: 'She is unsinkable'... Until a sub is classed, tested, and proven it should not be used for commercial deep dive operations," Rob Mcallum, leading deep sea exploration specialist, said.[2]

This was not rule breaking. This was laws of physics breaking, and there comes a point where you move from being a maverick to being a dangerous risk. He didn't just ignore them, he flaunted his disregard for safety.

"At some point, safety just is pure waste."

—STOCKTON RUSH[3]

While this case was ongoing, a lot of things started coming out in the news about the corners the CEO had cut, and many videos of him seeming to scoff in the face of experts on the subject of deep ocean submarine diving, as well as safety protocols put in place to protect people if something did in fact go wrong.

It turned out, January 18, 2018, OceanGate employee David Lochridge forwarded to the company's leaders an engineering report he had authored that was critical of OceanGate's research and development process for the Titan, according to lawsuits Lochridge and OceanGate filed against one another that year.[4] Lochridge was concerned about the materials used in the hull and a lack of testing performed on the hull to measure its ability to withstand the intense pressures of deep waters. In a video that saw a lot of play during the incident; the CEO is heard admitting that "I think I've broken them with logic and good engineering behind me. Carbon fiber and titanium? There's a rule you don't do that... Well, I did."[5]

After his email, the company had a meeting to discuss Lochridge's concerns. At the end of the meeting, Lochridge stated clearly he could not accept OceanGate's design decisions and would not authorize any crewed voyage without further testing. He was fired.

Remember how I have said know where your line is and know when you are willing to walk away? This line is good to have. I won't sign off on anything that will get someone killed. The other lesson here is don't ignore your experts when they are telling you something might be wrong.

OceanGate filed the lawsuit against Lochridge in June and July of 2018, alleging he had discussed confidential information with at least two other people. Lochridge countersued in

August 2018, denying that and claiming that OceanGate's lawsuit was an effort to discourage "whistleblowers from coming forth with quality control issues and safety concerns that threaten the safety of innocent passengers." Here is the thing: OceanGate's lawsuit to keep things quiet seems to have worked, as there was almost nothing online about the safety issues until the Titan incident.

There are times when the "I told you so" is something you never wish you will have to say.

The Titan case is an example of what not to do when you are metagaming or looking for ways to innovate and be a game changer. Don't ignore warnings. Don't think physics doesn't apply to you. Understand on a deep level *why* certain rules are in place, why certain things are done a certain way, before you decide to try to change them.

This isn't only true for rules like the physics on a submarine, but also the limits to what AI can actually do, brakes on the new car your company is building, that lithium battery fires can't be put out with a normal extinguisher, and that the human body can't work eighty-hour weeks indefinitely. You might think, sitting in a corporate space, that you don't have these sorts of rules to worry about, but I assure you they are there.

AXES AND ROOFTOPS

Now, let's look at defying standard practices from the angle of something that was successful. In other words, breaking protocol rules in a way that saved lives instead of losing them.

A lot of things went wrong for the city of New Orleans during Hurricane Katrina and in the aftermath, but the one that made international news was when the levels broke and flooded a major part of the city. This flooding left thousands stranded in their homes or on the rooftops of various other buildings throughout the area.

Urban search and rescue at this scale was something the Coast Guard had never done. Yes, they had dealt with urban flooding in some areas, but nothing of this magnitude with so many people trapped. Let's add a little more danger to the situation. Multiple storms were brewing in the Atlantic that could come crashing down on the city, making a bad situation worse. In fact, Hurricane Rita hit twenty-six days after Katrina.

In the days following the storms, as the rescues picked up tempo, the rescue swimmers found that many people had gone to their attics to escape the flood and had no way to get out. The waters didn't recede as quickly as some had hoped, and it was August in Louisiana. Quickly, these attics were becoming death traps.

At this point, the Coast Guard Rescue swimmers grabbed axes. The story is told by Aviation Survival Technician Second Class (AST2) Joel Sayers.

On the first day of rescue operations, [Sayers] was lowered onto a rooftop to rescue an older woman stranded by the rising floodwater. The noise and constant downward pressure coming from the helicopter was familiar, but the sloped roof and flying shingles were a new experience. When he landed, Sayers began talking to the frightened woman and learned that her husband was still in the attic of their house, unable to move. Sayers looked through the small opening in the roof the woman had managed to escape through and saw the woman's husband. After several failed attempts to widen the hole and free the man using the helicopter's crash ax, Sayers knew he needed something with more weight and strength if he was to save the man trapped inside.

Sayers looked through the hole in the roof and promised the man he would come back to get him. Sayers tied a brightly colored piece of cloth around one of the house's vent pipes to identify it because even with Global Positioning System everything looked the same. He then convinced the wife she had to—at least for now—leave her husband behind. With the wife aboard, the helicopter proceeded to a drop off point with a fire truck present, and a fire axe was obtained. The helicopter and crew returned to the house with the wife on board. Sayers was again lowered to the roof, looked through the hole, asked the husband to back away and began to chop a hole large enough to get him out. Once the man was removed from the attic, he was hoisted into the helicopter and reunited with his wife.[6]

This incident was explained to the rest of the responders the moment the helo returned to base, and immediately, Coasties from ATC Mobile contacted the managers of the closed Lowes and Home Depot stores in the area and made arrangements to purchase all of the axes and small chain saws they had. All helicopters were thereafter equipped with axes and/or power saws. The Coast Guard had never this done—going onto rooftops and having a swimmer use an axe to break in.

Doing this was potentially unsafe for all sorts of reasons: the rotor wash from the helo, the way the swimmer had to stand on the roof, the risk of hitting the people under the roof. So the Coast Guard quickly worked up some basic safety protocols that everyone was briefed on before they went out with the axes and chainsaws.

They didn't ask for permission to use the axes and wait for the heads of the aviation safety organizations to get back to them on whether they could or couldn't do the action. They just did it. They applied the knowledge they had from other emergencies, plus the knowledge of physics every pilot is expected to have, plus the skills and knowledge of the swimmers on how to maintain control of dangerous situations, and mixed them all together for a solution that saved lives. If you had asked swimmers and pilots in the months before, they would have explained to you how that isn't how things are done, how that is so dangerous. But some situations demand change, and they demand it without a committee meeting.

Now, I know these are very different situations, and I am not comparing them against each other specifically. I am outlining them as two very different situations around rule-breaking and innovating.

To whit, you cannot effectively innovate on a system without a full, deep understanding of the rules and why things are done the way they are done. Innovating or bending the rules, awesome. Breaking them? Best of luck to you. There can be valid reasons a thing is done in a certain way, so if you are going to change how the thing is done, you need to address the reasons directly or someone, at best, is going to lose a lot of money, or at worst, lose their life. So, before you go and rewrite rules, ask yourself:

- Why is this rule in place?
- Why do we engage in this activity in this way?
- Does it actually need to be changed?
- Why?
- No seriously, why? If the answer is because you want to, or you know you are right, you better be able to back it up with data.

To think you know more than everyone else in your field is foolish; to have figured out something they haven't yet is divine. Don't simply look at the rules and think, *Fuck those rules, I'm a rebel.* Instead, look at the rules, understand why they are the way they are, and then look for the blank spaces, the gaps, the places where no one has gone before.

Maverick always knew exactly what his plane could do at the very edges of physics and wasn't afraid to push those limits, and your limits likely don't involve a possible fiery explosion or having to eject out of a spiraling fighter plane, right? So be brave!

CHAPTER 9

Two Faces of Hubris

At my taekwondo school growing up, we always joked about the "look at me faceplant," which was a phenomenon every student experienced in their first class after obtaining their blackbelt. All of us did something embarrassing—falling on a basic kick, forgetting a form, or getting popped in the face by a junior belt while we were trying to do something showy sparring.

Why did this happen to so many—if not all—of us? We had gotten cocky. We had just passed the biggest test you could take; having a black belt made you a badass who would do anything. You were the expert. You were unstoppable. So, to a one, we had let our egos, which were at the moment puffed up beyond belief, get the better of us and had stopped looking at the basics. I have seen this problem repeated by people as they get promotions, or agencies like the Coast Guard who have been "successful" for so long doing what they do that they forget the basics and fall on their faces.

There has been a lot of research into what hubris is and what causes it, and no consensus on if it is good or bad. Spoiler alert: like most things, it depends on how you use it.

THE DARK SIDE

If you ask me one word to describe a lot of leadership of the Coast Guard, I would say it is hubris. Unfortunately, that hubris, specifically the pride the Coast Guard leadership takes in being able to do the impossible, to do more with less, has arguably resulted in a lot of the problems the Coast Guard faces today—an aging fleet, retention issues, and a budget that means the Coast Guard Base in Seattle still works out of offices where the pipes have lead and a number of the buildings are borderline condemned.

Let me put the lesson the USCG taught me here in very plain terms: being too proud to ask for help or speak up when there is an issue will eventually cause you a lot of problems. Even when you are a badass who can handle all the things, you are going to need to know when to suck up the ego and get assistance.

Hubris has a darker side I have to warn you about—hubris that you are above reproach, that you can do no wrong, or that you can cover up issues and no one will ever find out. I am sure those of you reading this are thinking I am going to talk about something like the takeover of Twitter, or an Amazon story, but the best example I can give of this is a story that broke while I was writing this book.[1]

In June of 2023, CNN broke a story about Operation Fouled Anchor, a secret investigation that not only brought to light decades of sexual assault at the US Coast Guard Academy but also put a spotlight on a disturbing cover-up. The CNN report exposed how the commandant of the US Coast Guard, and his leadership team at the time, deliberately concealed the startling findings of the investigation despite earlier pledges to bring the matter to light. As a woman who left the Academy in 1997 for let's just say, several reasons, the findings of the investigation did not surprise me, and the cover-up infuriated me.

It bears repeating: despite internal records indicating the team that worked on the investigation had mapped out plans to brief Congress and Department of Homeland Security (DHS) officials, meaning it would have become public record, the command at the time opted to withhold the report's outcomes. The following command also didn't say anything about the investigation until CNN broke the story.[2]

When I saw the letter the commandant at the time had written to the field about the investigation and the actions they were taking, I hadn't seen the news breaking about it.[3] At first, I cried because I was like, *Finally! Finally, they are doing something. Finally, they are listening and believing! About time!* Then I saw the letter had been a reaction to the news that was breaking; they weren't being proactive, this was a reaction to being called out on something that had been covered up. The testimony given before Congress was damning, and I am sure by the time this book comes out, even more will have come to light. Here is a sample of the testimony:

"Too often, Coast Guard Senior Leaders have punished junior officers, mid-grade officers, and enlisted members for their "misdeeds" but have failed to police themselves. Too many times, Senior Leaders have interceded, overturning recommendations—and at times, convictions—made by independent parties. Senior Leaders

have also permitted members to quietly resign or retire in lieu of receiving punishment or adverse documentation. For members who are able to quietly retire, they are subsequently afforded military honors and a fully funded government pension. This double standard is simply unacceptable. If this institution is to change, Senior Leaders must first be loyal to the Coast Guard rather than to themselves."

—MELISSA K. MCCAFFERTY[4]

So the assaults in the first place were ignored or covered up, the investigation was kept secret, and then the results were covered up for almost 6 years. Now, I understand keeping the investigation classified while it was happening, as you want to avoid witness tampering or intimidation as some of the men implicated were in positions of power in the service. But to cover up the findings? That is unforgivable, and the hubris to think that not only was it the right choice but it would never come out? That's unfathomable to me.

This is an example of hubris syndrome on the part of Coast Guard leadership, to be honest. Hubris syndrome is associated with power, more likely to manifest itself the longer the person exercises power and the greater the power they exercise. This syndrome, as described by the Royal College of Physicians, is not a mental illness or brain damage, and tends to go away once someone is no longer in power.[5]

THE BENEFIT OF HUBRIS

The thing is, hubris isn't entirely a bad thing. Research has shown that hubris in executives leads to more innovation in their companies.[6] Honestly, there are times when the hubris demonstrated in the Coast Guard actually saves lives.

Sometimes that works to the benefit of the service; there are a plethora of examples about the Coast Guard doing gutsy stuff in the face of impossible odds. Look at Hurricane Katrina, or watch the case of the *SS Pendleton* rescue mission—the movie *The Finest Hours* with Chris Pine (2016) is based on these events, which occurred in 1952 off the coast of Cape Cod, Massachusetts.

Imagine a time when epic mustaches were as plentiful as seagulls on the beach and sailors' hats made them look like Popeye cosplayers. It's 1952, and a huge nor'easter is smashing up the coast of Cape Code like Godzilla. Out in the midst of this aquatic mosh pit is the *SS Pendleton*, a massive oil tanker that's suddenly doing its best impression of Humpty Dumpty, if Humpty Dumpty were an oil tanker that had snapped itself in two. The crew of the *Pendleton* were in a hell of a situation, clinging to the back half of their broken ship like barnacles on a buoy.

Cue the dramatic music and zoom in on Bernie Webber, a dashing Coast Guardsman with a Massachusetts accent that would make Mark Wahlberg proud and the embodiment of the motto "You must go out, you don't have to come back." (He just ignored that second part.) The crew included a mechanic who was practically married to his wrench and a newbie sailor who got greener than a sea sick sea cucumber. It's like assembling a squad of oddball Avengers, but with life jackets and a healthy respect of dodging seagull poop.

Waves as tall as skyscrapers? Check. Wind that could blow the whiskers off a walrus? Check. A bar that could flip them over faster than a card sharp flips a winning hand? Oh yeah. Don't let the name fool you. It's not a cozy pub where sailors have been telling sea stories over a pint for years; crossing the treacherous Chatham Bar is something that, even with today's modern self-righting vessels, you have to go through serious training before you are allowed to traverse. The Chatham Bar is a sandy, shifting nightmare that's been the bane of sailors and ships alike for centuries. It moves with the tides, rearranging its contours faster than you'd think possible, and creates water vortexes that just wait to whip a ship around. One moment, you think you've got it all figured out, and the next, your ship's doing the cha-cha with the ocean floor, and you're left praying to Poseidon for mercy.

These Coasties were trained, knew the sea, and had hubris in spades. They navigated the treacherous waters and managed rogue waves, and I like to picture them cussing into the wind that nobody can hear because, well, it's really windy. The question beating at them like a drum: will they make it in time? But like a determined dolphin, Webber maneuvered the thirty-six-foot lifeboat under *Pendleton*'s stern. The crew, trapped in the stern section, abandoned the wreck of their ship into the Coast Guard motor lifeboat. The crew of that Coast Guard boat saved thirty-two of the thirty-three crew members that day.

Only a certain personality type wants to go out when others are battening down the hatches. When the weather gets too shitty for anyone in their right mind to leave their house, the

Coast Guard is there charging into the waves to help those in need. It's one of the best, and worst, things about us. While there is a healthy respect for the sea and the training we need to have to do our jobs, there is a certain hubris to look into the face of a Category 3 or 4 storm and say "Fuck you."

Making this story even crazier? A second ship was out there that had also cracked in half, the *SS Fort Mercer*. So, what did those Coasties do? They turned right around and did it again, with a little help from CGC Yakutat and CGC Acushnet.

There are two sides to the hubris coin: one being that you can accomplish great things, the other being that too much of it can lead you to make some pretty serious mistakes.

HOW TO TELL THE DIFFERENCE

So how do you balance it? Well, look at the two stories I have told in this chapter. One was about doing something in order to save lives. The other? While I don't know the reasons the command made the decision they did, evidence suggests they weren't making the decision based on what was right for the victims, their families, or the Coast Guard at large.

Let that be your guiding light. Why are you making the decision you are making? It isn't bad if it is being made out of hubris, but what is the core thing you are trying to accomplish? Is the hubris coming from a place of you knowing your skills and what a badass you are, or from a place of privilege due to your rank/gender and thinking no one can touch you? Because trust me, on that second one, they can touch you and it's going to hurt when they do.

So, you are about to make a proposal to your boss that seems crazy and will cost a lot of money, or you want to make a massive change to a process at your company that if it fails could cost millions—you know, something that gives you that adrenaline spike, knots in the stomach, this could be risky feeling. How can you tell if you are on the light side or the dark side of hubris?

Ask yourself a few basic questions. Seriously write down answers for these.

1. Why am I doing this? What is my real motivation?
2. Who will this help?
3. Who will this hurt?
4. What is the cost of this decision if it goes wrong?
5. What is the reward if it goes right?

If the reward doesn't outweigh the cost, why are you doing it? If it is going to hurt more people, you are probably on the wrong side of hubris. If you are doing it for unethical or morally questionable reasons, let alone illegal ones, you are on the wrong side of hubris. If you are doing it to save face, that one is going to be up to you, but as I have mentioned, saving face rarely pays off in the long run.

Everyone has their personal morals and ethics they work within, but remember, at the end of the day, no matter which side of hubris you end up on, you have to live with that decision. So ask yourself, can you live with the fallout, good or bad?

CHAPTER 10

Rotations Make the World Go Round

I managed to keep anyone from crying, screaming, or otherwise losing their shit in one of the most stressful environments in tech—AWS re:Invent's launch operations room. I also helped various service teams within AWS keep their teams from burning out during the company's COVID-19 response. I get asked all the time how I keep myself or my teams from burning out in high-visibility, high-stress situations. Besides the snarky response of "Look, literally no one was going to die in the launch room," answer is this:

Rotations, redundancies, and ridiculousness.

ROTATION ISN'T JUST SOMETHING PLANET EARTH DOES.

People can only work at a certain stress level or operational tempo for so long before something is going to give, either their mind or their body. While everyone's threshold is different for what they can sustain, literally everyone has their breaking point, no matter what the Elon Musk's of the world say.

In the Coast Guard, there are various types of watch rotations. On a ship, for example, you are on four-hour rotations. In a command center, the watch rotations at most units are twelve hours, so you will be on from 6:00 a.m. to 6:00 p.m., and then the 6:00 p.m. to 6:00 a.m. rotation.

There are even rules for civilians on ships. 46 USCG 8104(b) says licensed crewmembers on vessels less than 100 GT on coastwise or ocean voyages are not required to work more than twelve hours in one day.[1] The reason for all of these set rotations is to optimize operations while minimizing the risk of mistakes or fatal errors. Airline pilots have similar rules and regulations around how many flights they can do and how much sleep they need to get.

So, one of the things I did with my launch team, and then advised service teams on during COVID-19, was set up a similar system of watch rotations. First, let me explain how a watch rotation works and then how you can apply it to your team without having to hire a whole bunch of extra head count. Trust me, I know how stupidly hard it can be to get head count in good years, let alone in a post-pandemic world that still hasn't made up its mind on how it wants to work.

When you are getting ready for watch, the first thing you want is coffee. Okay, that's not true for everyone, but you need to make sure you are on your game, not distracted, and ready to intake information from the off-going watch. Then, at a set time *before* your watch is due to start, you make contact with the off-going watch. In the case of a ship, you go up to the bridge, or in a command duty center, you go into the secure space.

You aren't there to catch up on the latest hockey scores or what insanity happened on social media; you are there to get a pass-down of set specific information. This information is standard so nothing is forgotten or left out. Often, there are check sheets for remembering things, but they also grill you into memorizing the list so you can not only remember what to ask but retain what you are told.

I really don't recommend trying to make your people memorize pass-downs for their jobs. Instead, come up with a quick check sheet on information that needs to be passed between people. I do strongly recommend you make sure people do these pass-downs face to face—either on a video call or in person—and not over email, as context can be lost and questions can get delayed responses.

So you do the pass-down with the relevant information for the oncoming watch and the off-going watch departs. This isn't departing and you can just call them up with questions; this is they leave and, unless something is about to explode or burn down, you leave them alone for their recovery time.

How does this work in the private sector where rotations won't be twelve hours? One of the toughest things to work out for team rotations during the COVID-19 response was determining how much time teams could be working and how much they needed off. You see, unlike being on watch rotations at a command center where you will have a few days on and then a few off, there is a lot of work to be done at a company where the modern workplace isn't set up for that sort of watch.

Also, I should point out that I am talking about using rotations not necessarily for everyday work but for critical work like a massive event, a crisis response, or crunch time before a product is due.

So, let's say you have a sudden influx of customers wanting a product due to an emerging issue like COVID-19, and they shift to everything being online. Human nature is both that everyone is going to want to help and also no one wants to be left out of the hot shit—the things that are exciting and or can make for incredible career bullets after the fact. So right out of the gate, everyone is going to want to go all in and go as hard as they can. Never sleep, never surrender!

That mentality is a recipe for breakdowns and mistakes.

So what you need to do is set up a rotation. This means a certain number of your team will be assigned to the response, while others focus on the usual daily tasks. You know, the normal stuff of running the business, keeping customers who are maybe standard users happy too. You have a set amount of time that folks are working on the tough thing, and then they do a pass-down and rotate to do something "normal." Side note: this can also be used as a way to deal with a super toxic customer or partner over the long term to keep your people from getting emotional burnout. I mean, if you can't get rid of the customer/partner, that is—as in not working with them anymore. Geez, this isn't that type of military pointers book.

Before you start building your rotations, there are some questions to ask yourself:

- **How long will this go on?** You need to take a serious look and determine how long you think the issue will last. Is this a product launch that will be done in six months or a major event? Or is this something like COVID-19 where you really don't know how long it is going to take?
- **How long does the work needed take?** Is this something as simple as "flipping some switches," or is there going to be onboarding support needed? Follow-up support?
- **How many people on your team can do the needed work?** This is honestly simply so you figure out how many rotations you can do. Ugh. Math time!

Having two rotations is great; having three is even better. Why? Because redundancies will save your ass. Have a backup for your backup, especially because shit happens. Not OMG COVID-19-level shit, but kids get sick, people quit; all sorts of things can come up.

Now, how do you decide how long the rotations should last? This part will vary the most from team to team, so I really can't say what will work for you. Here are a few questions I used to figure out the different rotations for the service teams when I did it.

- How long does it usually take to get someone with no experience onboarded to this service?
- When, in normal circumstances, is the first dip in support needed? Like when they seem to really get it and not need as much guidance?
- Is your team used to working in sprints? How long are those sprints?

If this doesn't help you then I will tell you that the rotations I worked out usually were one to two weeks, but almost never more than two.

I know, I know. How are you going to explain the rotations to your teams, let alone to your management? Honestly, if this is a crisis situation or a major issue situation, I have a feeling most management and personnel will be happy to have guidance through the insanity. If there are still questions, explain that there is a standard for watch rotations that has been used for a very long time to maintain safety for everything from ships to planes, to operating heavy machinery.

Here is the deal for in the workplace: a rotation minimizes burnout; it gives people a time where they literally will sleep better because they aren't being woken up or doing late-night calls—or like me, will give themselves a break from obsessing.

If the empathetic reasoning doesn't work then there is the straight-up fact that after working at a certain tempo for too long, people start to make mistakes. The longer you go without a break, the more likely you are to make cascading mistakes and could actually make the problem worse. Bringing in a new rotation on the project also puts fresh eyes on it, eyes that have a higher likelihood of catching problems that might have been missed.

And if your boss is a true soul-sucking despot who couldn't care less about people and only cares about the bottom line, this system will allow you to sustain a high level of work from everyone over a longer period of time.

Here are some of the signs you need to start thinking about putting rotations into place:

1. High performing employees missing deadlines.
2. Work begins to include a lot of errors.
3. Hours go well above a standard forty a week for more than five weeks in a row.
4. Employees start working on what is supposed to be time off regularly.

While you might not be flying a plane, mistakes can add up to cost a lot. While I will talk about the personnel cost of crunch time and a lack of breaks in Chapter 13, understanding how to create sustainable rotations is what will save you from the cost both to your employees' health and your bottom line. If you have software engineers working on lines of code that are not at the top of their game, they can make errors that could take down your entire system.

I can hear some of you saying, "But, Ana, we work in Agile, and rotations won't work for that." In fact, they do work very well in the Agile system. As Team A is going through a sprint, Team B is keeping track and working alongside, while Team C is focusing on what is coming up next and getting things ready. Then they rotate for the next sprint, with Team B taking the lead so A can get a break to work on something else.

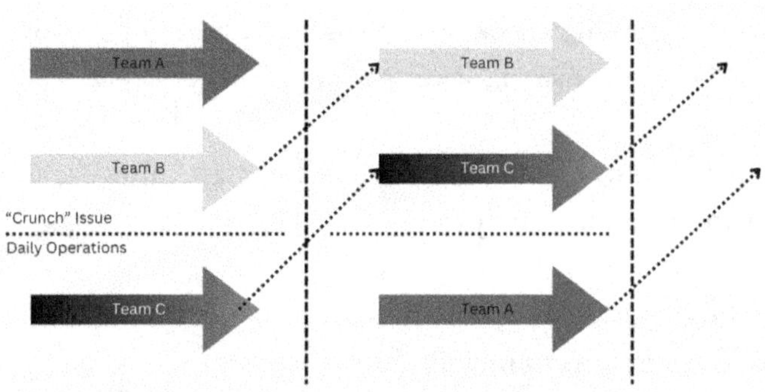

So before you say, "Oh, this would be too expensive. There is no way they would let me do rotations on my team," I challenge you to look at ways you might be able to implement some sort of rotation or flexibility to protect your people from burnout. Used in conjunction with some redundancies and ridiculousness, you might find yourself knocking those quarterly goals out of the park with a team that would walk through fire for you, instead of wanting to light you on fire.

CHAPTER 11

Let's Get Redundant

When we tell someone they are being redundant, it is usually not meant in a complimentary way. The thing is, redundancies in your operations will save your ass. Sometimes redundancies are all that stand between you and some pretty epic failures. I will be discussing two types of redundancies in this section. Let's start with the bits and bytes example, literal system redundancies.

Let me take a moment to tell you the harrowing tale of the Coast Guard heath records system debacle. You know how, when you go to the doctor, they pull up your records and have all this information about you, your medical history? It is pretty important for your doctor to have easy access to, right?

WHOOPS, LOST ALL YOUR DATA...

In 2010, the Coast Guard started working on replacing its aging Electronic Health Records (EHR) system with a suite of modernized systems they named the Integrated Health Information System (IHiS). The intention was to modernize various healthcare services and provide additional functions, including a document management system and better integration with the Department of Defense systems. This second piece was critical due to how small the Coast Guard is. At many duty stations, service members rely on the DoD medical system because the Coast Guard base they work at has no facilities.

In 2015, the Coast Guard announced the modernization project would be canceled. According to the GAO report[1], as of August 2017, $59.9 million was spent on the project over nearly seven years, and no equipment or software could be reused for future efforts. That's right, they had spent that much money on a system so bad absolutely none of it was going to be usable.

Sit with that for a moment. How would you explain to your boss that you spent $60 million and have absolutely nothing to show for it? Scary, right? Oh, it gets better, or, well, worse, if you want to be technical about it.

That's right. The Coast Guard had to revert to paper medical records because the legacy system and health IT support systems were retired in January 2016. They did not continue the contract for the old system, not knowing when the new system would be online. This means a lot of us who got out of the service in the 2015–2016 have incomplete or completely missing records.

Even though all of our medical records were supposed to have been printed before we left, I can tell you from personal experience that did not happen. I was given my paper medical file and told I needed to photocopy it. That's twelve years of my medical records that now had huge holes wherever nothing on paper was added because it was only in digital format. This lack of planning ahead means there is no way to disprove that something happened to them medically while in the service, so it could lead to potential lawsuits over loss of benefits due to the error.

What in the flying hell happened? The tale is one of mismanagement of epic proportions, but if you asked me or any of my tech peers, it boils down to having people in a decision-making capacity who, at a fundamental level, do not understand technology or the processes by which you build a new product.

I am not talking about waterfall versus scrum; I am talking about how to gather the minimum requirements a product needs—and then actually stick to them. I am talking about knowing the difference between the various back-end technologies to make a project like this work.

In another chapter, I talk about what the Coast Guard taught me about tech debt and the impacts of leadership that grows up in a vacuum.

REDUNDANCY ISN'T A WASTEFUL EXPENSE

This all leads up to the lesson of: redundancy will save your ass. Sure, it would not have gotten the Coast Guard back the tens of millions wasted, but it would have saved the "customers" of the system from having their data go flying off into the great darkness of data loss land, never to be recovered.

The lesson here isn't just don't turn off one system until the other system is up and running. It's also important that not only is the new system running but it has been online long enough to ensure it is stable. At minimum, six months is my default parallel running time.

If we take another lesson from the Coast Guard: pretty much anyone else who is going to stand watch on the bridge knows how to read a nautical chart, even on the new cutters that have all the latest GPS mapping technology (she types chuckling to herself because the latest means whatever was the shiny new thing when the ship was commissioned, not what someone in the tech world might call the latest. No AI making helm decisions here, folks). When, inevitably some brand-new ensign or seaman asks why they have to learn all this doing it by hand chart work, the answer is always:

"Just in case the system goes down."

You see, when out to sea, GPS can get wonky in different parts of the world; storms can mess with satellite connectivity or what latitude you are at. Let's just say the Arctic and the Antarctic are not places you are going to be watching a bunch of TikToks. So there are all sort of reasons to have other methods for navigating even before you consider anything that comes with warfare or damage to the ship itself. So, learning how to do things on paper is essential.

Now let's talk about the other part of redundancies: people. Having people on your team who can backstop others means that if someone "falls out," for any reason, you don't have a complete system failure. Have you ever been working on a project and either someone who needs to take time off "just can't" because they are the only one who can do their part of a project? Or they do take time off or get sick and the project grinds to a halt?

Wherever you can, try to arrange backups on their projects where at least someone knows how to pick up their work if they have to step away for some reason. Not only you, by the way, because I don't care what you think, you can't be the backup for everyone on your team. Stop trying to be a hero. This way, if the worst happens, you have someone who can carry on.

Yes, yes. There are always roles where having a backup isn't possible. No, you don't get a spare CEO, but if you don't think that CEO has different parts of their operations backed up by each of their directs so they can, in fact, have time to, you know, sleep, eat, scroll social media while sitting on the toilet, you are crazy. And no, you can't take a developer who has only worked in Scala and throw them into a project that needs Java and PHP with no additional training. That's just crazy pants. But, wherever it is possible, having maximum transparency between teams can be monumental for getting through chaotic, difficult times.

Now, there is a behavior pattern we see in a lot of American companies: gatekeeping information to appear more relevant. Often, this is driven by the thought that if there are others around who can do what you do, then you are at higher risk of getting let go or less likely to get promoted.

I am not talking about having everyone on your team know how to do what everyone else can do; think of it as having transparency in operations. Having one person who is the only one who knows where things are or how certain things work is setting your team up for burnout and failure. And trust me, as you implement a system of redundancy, you will find very quickly who your bottlenecks are and if they are intentionally being a single source on purpose.

RIPPLE EFFECT CAN BRING EVERYTHING TO A HALT

Let's look at air travel. In August of 2023, Federal Aviation Administration (FAA) extended a limited waiver on minimum usage requirements for slots used by airlines at New York and Washington, DC, area airports.[2] The extension came, in part, due to shortages in air traffic control (ATC) staff. The issue was pervasive and with a reduced number of controllers, which resulted in a limited ability of the FAA to regulate and maintain airspace. Limited airspace control staff meant limited planes could fly at any given time. At the time of the extension, the FAA was understaffed by three thousand people.

According to the FAA, the availability of factor "accounted for time controllers can't cover traffic demand." This could be due to leave, training, or additional off-site activities.[3] Disagreements between organizations and within the FAA itself over appropriate staffing levels without reconciliation limit the ability for the FAA to implement a change in its workforce plan.

Add to that the FAA uses a system called Cru-X/ART for workforce management. It records and tracks the time controllers spend at their positions because, similar to pilots, there are restrictions to how long they can work. Problem is, similar to the Coast Guard health care system not communicating with the DoD system, the current scheduler and Cru-X/ART system did not communicate well with each other. There is a replacement for the current Cru-X system called the Air Traffic Operations Management System (ATOMS), but as of October 2023, there was not a set date for when the new system would be in place.[4]

So there are multiple redundancy issues going on for the FAA. They don't have enough air traffic controllers to cover shifts let alone handle a crisis if it arises, making for a system ripe for failure. The Office of the Inspector General put together a report on this that ended in some recommendations. "1) Complete a comprehensive review of the model for distribution of certified professional controllers (CPC) for air traffic control facilities and update interim CPC staffing levels as necessary and 2) Implement a new labor distribution system that includes features such as timekeeping, overtime and Controller-in-Charge tracking, and real-time leave balances."[5]

During the time that these issues have been happening, flight delays are up from 16.78 percent (2021) to 22.52 percent (2023), according to the Bureau of Transportation Statistics. Fun fact, there are actually less planes flying in 2023 than there were in 2021 due to pilot shortages with the airlines and other cuts.

What does this result in? A lot of pissed off travelers, burned out air traffic controllers, and frustrated pilots. Luckily, due to federal safety regulations, the lack of personnel redundancy has not resulted in anyone getting hurt.

Of course, this is a dramatic example, but having backups can mean the difference between success and utter failure. Imagine if cloud providers didn't have backup regions for their backup regions, so if one goes down, the internet crashes and you can't get to Amazon?

HOW TO BUILD REDUNDANCIES

That's a lot of examples of why redundancies are important, but how do you set about building a system with backups without getting your ass chewed by your boss for "waste."

LAY THE GROUNDWORK

1. Identify the risks if you don't have redundancy. Call out all the money it could cost your company in hours spent, customer impact, and possible lawsuits if there is a failure due to the lack of backup.
2. Identify the easiest ways to create redundancies—cross training? Running a system in parallel?
3. If you really want to get the point across, show the cost difference between what will happen if there is a failure versus just having backups.

GET TO BUILDING

1. Sit down with your team and explain what you plan to do, and why it is important. This is critical because your team needs to be bought in; they need to understand why

what you are doing is important and why it isn't a threat to their jobs. Remember that mindset of, *I am only as important to the company as the information I keep to myself.*

2. Set up shadow time. Have team members spend a little time shadowing each other to learn about projects or tasks. Make sure you let your team know this is a part of their job. This is important to get around the inevitable complaint of "But I have things to get done!"

3. Find a way to reward team members for doing the work of learning about each other, and emphasize to them why knowing more is better for all of their careers. Knowledge being power and all that.

4. If you are looking for redundancies in systems you are working on, check your contracts to make sure there is no gap between the old and the new.

This sort of thing isn't easy, especially in a world where most companies are looking at where to cut out any extra costs. Instead, lean into the other things most companies are looking at—risk reduction.

That's enough talking about leaning into your boss's nightmares to get the right thing done. Sometimes you have to be the sword and shield to get things done, but let's take a deep breath and talk next about being the balloon animal instead.

CHAPTER 12

Live, Love, Laugh at Yourself

Look, I am not saying you should wear a clown nose to do open heart surgery, but for the love of dogs, stop taking everything so seriously. It isn't just crisis or "being in the trenches" of crunch that bonds a team, or keeps them from breaking. Some sort of humor, little stupid things, always come out at these times. Silly nicknames like being called The Ensign no matter what rank I reached in the Coast Guard, realizing you have eaten ten pounds of sour patch kids in four days together when someone complains they can't taste anything anymore… Those are the moments that keep people grounded and give them an outlet to bring the pressure down.

Finding fun ways for your team to step away from the chaos and drama for a bit can do wonders for the morale and health of your team. If you don't give people positive outlets, they will find others, such as excessive drinking. They also might not relax at all and then you are going to end up with tired, hangry people probably looking for other jobs on their cellphones at their desk.

You might be surprised that learning how to have fun as a leader and help a team relax is something that the Coast Guard taught me. Well, let me say that when you are stuck on a floating metal box where every waking hour could be nothing but work, finding a way for people to let off a little steam and relax becomes incredibly important. It isn't only for morale; it is literally to keep people's brains sharp and their wits about them.

A study from the University of Essex showed that "participants who tried to relax and follow their hobbies recorded an average well-being boost of 8 percent and a 10 percent drop in stress and anxiety."[1] The study also showed, across three countries, people who prioritized achievement over enjoyment were less happy on the next day.

HURRICANE LEISURE SUITS

Let me tell you about hurricane leisure suits and flip flops. After Hurricane Katrina came Hurricane Rita to roll right over the top of the already devastated area. Two folks I had only just met, Tippets and Lutz, were deployed with a team in the field that was being evacuated out of the path of the storm. Somehow, their duffles with their uniforms went to Huntville, AL, and they ended up in Alexandria, LA, with the rest of us. So lacking coveralls and given a small stipend to get some clothes, they went off in the scant hours before the storm to see if anything was open.

Now, these two fine young men could have looked for the local Walmart—which I am not sure ever closes for anything. Seriously, it could be the apocalypse and Walmart would still be there saying, "Save Money. Live Better"—but instead, they happened upon a thrift store. To this day, one of them claims they looked for a thrift store and the other swears it was the only place they could find. They also could have snagged some jeans and a shirt, cargo shorts, or anything like that. What they came back to the command post in? Velvet suits. I am talking about maroon and dark green, wide lapeled slightly bell-bottomed velvet suits torn out of the 70s. With flip flops.

They seriously came back to the place where they were likely to run into the Federal On Scene Coordinator, any number of admirals, looking like they were ready to disco down the hallways. When I talked to them about including this story and picture in the book, they laughed and were surprised to hear how much that moment influenced me. Sometimes situations are hard and ridiculous, and being a little ridiculous can make everything better. I didn't have to take myself so seriously all the time.

They never got in trouble for running around out of uniform like that. In fact, it was something almost everyone got a laugh out of no matter their rank. Everyone who saw them gave them a hard time, and looked a little brighter for that moment of unexpected levity.

I took this lesson very much to heart and have a bit of a reputation for wearing shirts that say—thematically appropriate—ridiculous things to work. On my last day in the Coast Guard, I showed up to headquarters without my uniform, wearing a T-shirt that quoted Seahawk Marshawn Lynch. "I'm just here so I don't get fined." At AWS, I would arrive to meetings wearing shirts that said "Not enough coffee or middle fingers for today," or other such silliness to get a laugh out of my peers.

Even if they expect you to wear suits, unless you are testifying in front of Congress or on trial, why not wear some ridiculous socks or a tie that shows who you really are and might make someone else smile? The thing is, it isn't really just the clothes; it's about showing humor and humanity.

LOOK OUT FOR THE BLUE TURTLE SHELL

One of my favorite ways I ever brought a little fun to a situation would be having Mario Kart in the AWS Launch Operations room at re:Invent. I know, not the dramatic example you were expecting. Find me at a conference some time and reference this chapter. I will tell you the story of the roller skates in the Houma LA field command during the BP Oil spill.

So, Mario Kart in the Ops room. I had a set budget for the launch room, and the vendor just had to let me know what different things cost so I stayed on budget. Yes, there were necessities like tables, chairs, power strips, and everyone was demanding a computer monitor for their laptops. My priority was setting up a space people could work in for crazy hours without their asses going numb, them passing out, or them losing their shit.

I prioritized three things: making sure the chairs everyone was working from were comfortable for long hours, making sure the food wasn't just conference left overs whenever they could remember to feed us, and making sure there were comfy beanbag chairs and a huge TV screen over in the corner.

What was on that screen? Mario Kart. Then, when the first day kicked off, we made sure people knew that at any point outside of launch calls, there was Mario Kart and comfy chairs if they needed a break but didn't have time to go out of the room.

What I hadn't expected was how many ways people would take to playing the game or how many people would nap in those beanbags. Some people would just take a break and play. Then there were people who, when someone was getting bitchy, would tell their teammate—good-naturedly—to have a time out and point to the corner. One group couldn't decide where they were going for dinner that night after we were done, so the two choices each got a driver and they did a drive-off.

The beanbags, too, became places to relax and read a book, have a cup of coffee and chat with friends away from their desks, or read a book for a bit. I am pretty sure upon reading this, whoever has the picture of me zonked out and drooling on myself after a call will probably post it on social media for you to view. It's not pretty.

When it was time to be serious—on a launch call, for example—everyone snapped to and got business done. But when it was time for people to do the rest of the work, that time-out corner, as it came to be called, got the most positive feedback of anything I had set up in that room, hands down. Close behind it was my obsession with making sure there was really good comfort food catered in, and the incident with me dressing like I was auditioning for the Greatest Showman.

FIND THAT BALANCE

Yes, working is serious, especially when you are doing a launch, or a high profile event, but you have to look for the ways to find those small bits of humor of humanity in the work, or you are going to burn out your team and your people.

I am not saying you should start doing mandatory "fun" time with your team. In fact, a study by the University of Sydney has shown that team building exercises that are compulsory usually have the inverse effect of bonding the team, leaving many team members feeling resentful of leadership.[2]

So whatever you decide to do, it has to be voluntary, and I strongly recommend you do it during business hours, especially if your team works in person. I suggest this, quite simply, because people have lives outside of work, and resentment is more likely to build if they believe they have to do extra time outside of business hours in order to "fit in," which is especially difficult for single parents or those who have major outside of work obligations.

Here are some things I have found to be successful in having a little fun when working with teams remotely:

1. A daily question in the team channel. Keep the questions light, like "What was your favorite cartoon as a kid?" And never make it required to participate.
2. Instead of a one hour all hands where you talk all business, make the second half of the time a trivia team event or find a game that is work friendly. We played Fall Guys from Epic Games, as it was free to play, multiplatform, and people who had kids around could have them join.
3. Have a Wikiball tournament. Here is how it works.
   a. Everyone writes down two to three things they think you might find on Wikipedia. For example, Kentucky, Harrison Ford, and wine grapes.
   b. Everyone gets to a set starting page in Wikipedia.
   c. Pick someone at random to read one of their three things. Example, you started on page broccoli and the new topic is Harrison Ford.
   d. Using links on the page only, everyone tried to get to that new thing. In this case, the first person to get from broccoli to Harrison Ford wins.

e. Have the person who won read of their path what
   links they used to get to the win.

One of the things I love about Wikiball is how it shows everyone in the group how differently their minds work. No one ever takes the same links to get to the answers. If none of these work for you, try to find a game that works with your group type.

Just remember to check any games you might play for work appropriateness. Looking at you, Charty Party. Seriously, whoever came up with a game where you improve presentations off of random charts and graphs is a genius.

Find that time to be lighthearted, to demonstrate you have a sense of humor and are human, and encourage your people to do the same. It can do wonders for the team. This also ties back into a lot of what I talk about in other chapters about making sure people have enough of their own down time to do what they like.

CHAPTER 13

Crunch is for Cereal

So not all of the lessons I learned from the US Coast Guard were done by things they did right. In fact, the Coast Guard does a whole lot of stuff wrong. One of the most problematic things in the Coast Guard, as it is in many services, is the way it approaches alcohol. Specifically, though, I want to talk about port calls and how it applies to running a team that will likely never see a day at sea.

For those of you who have never seen the movies where sailors go crazy on a port call, or heard the jokes about sailors and their girls in every port, port calls are when a ship pulls into a port that isn't necessarily their home port.

UNDERWAY, UNDER PRESSURE

Basically, what happens is a ship will get underway for a certain amount of time, usually anywhere from three months to sometimes more than a year, depending on the size of the ship. The whole time, you are on this floating metal island with one hundred-plus of your closest friends. You are with the same people day in and day out that entire time, and depending on how the satellites are doing on any given day, you might not have connection enough to email your family.

This is a massive improvement from when I was a child when it was a delight to get a cassette tape from my dad talking to me and reading me stories, and maybe a couple letters, but it is still very isolating. You can't exactly just go for a walk, check out a movie, or visit a park.

Well, that's fine and all. But let's also add to this that the ships are dry. Dry ship means you don't drink when you're on the ship. And think about what happens to your body when you go three months without drinking any alcohol. You are now a freaking lightweight. All right now, also imagine you are trapped at work with no real breaks for three months straight.

Sure, there are mealtimes, and you do get to sleep, but you not get an opportunity to get out. Or you catch a movie with your wife. Anything to give you mental space from work. No respite. And then after three months of being penned up in a giant metal box, they pull into a port and let you loose to go have some time off the ship. They might warn you before you go to behave yourself.

Well, what happens is a lot of trouble. People get incredibly intoxicated. People get in fights. People do all sorts of inappropriate things. A lot of sexual assaults happen on port calls, as well as fights and other incidents. So, while we can't pen people up in their offices, especially for remote workers, you can, in fact, still be in an abusive work situation where you quite simply can't maintain the level of engagement they want you to, and it'll burn you out.

The thing being on a ship taught me about port calls is you have got to be incredibly careful when people are suddenly given access to an uncontrolled environment, especially one with alcohol. As a leader, you need to have a better work-life balance than making your people work themselves to death for three months in a row. The whiplash of surprise that comes with *Here's some free time, no rules, go forth and drink* is too much for most people.

In my discussions with friends in the video game industry, I found strange parallels in their "crunch" time to what it was like to be out to sea. Sleep schedules became a mess because everything was based on insane work schedules, families were rarely seen, and birthdays were missed. The things that made people active members of their family and friend groups were pushed to the side and health was ignored as those office buildings became much like a ship on the high sea.

When I talked about port calls and how problematic they were with a friend, he laughed and said it sounded a lot like E3 in its heyday.

E3 NO MORE

E3, which was cancelled in 2023, was once considered *the* big show to end all shows for the video game industry. It had been running since 1995 and was when major game studios would announce their big games coming up for the next year or more. New products were announced, like the Xbox Kinnect.

In 1995, the first E3 was one of the greatest cases of one-upmanship in video game history. Sega chose to reveal their brand-new console, the Saturn, completely out of the blue during their showcase and its heavy $399 price tag (about $796 dollars today.) So PlayStation president Steve Race got on stage to utter a single figure: "299." This kicked off Playstation dominating the industry for the next ten years by staying under the price of their biggest competitors.[1]

E3 was the place game developers knew if they could nail the trailer and announcement for their game, they could generate a huge appetite for their game and make presales skyrocket. This was the place where every big announcement lived, so you had to make sure your big announcement was bigger and shinier than all of your competition.

No pressure, right?

Then, once you hit the gate of announcing at E3, the race was on to produce the game on time no matter what because someone got on stage and promised a massive fan base of often volatile folks your game would be out the week after Thanksgiving or something.

Great. No pressure for that either, right?

While the Cambridge dictionary defines crunch time as "a point at which something difficult must be done:"[2] What the term has come to mean in the video game and tech industry is the period of time that no one sleeps, they work insane hours, they ignore their families, and they grind with no break to make sure the game gets launched on time. While some parts of the industry have gotten better through much discussion and a flood of journalists doing write ups of this company or that having a toxic culture, crunch is still a thing that happens far too often.

In 2019, a study 40 percent of game developers reported having worked in crunch time at least once over the course of the previous year.[3] If you thought that the pandemic would have calmed that crunch down because people were working from home, you'd be sadly disappointed. As game designer Glen Schofield demonstrated when he tweeted in 2022:

"I only talk about the game during an event. We r working six to seven days a week, nobody's forcing us. Exhaustion, tired, Covid but we're working. Bugs, glitches, perf fixes. One last pass thru audio. twelve to fifteen hr days. This is gaming. Hard work. Lunch, dinner working. U do it cause ya luv it."[4]

While Schofield removed the tweet, then apologized, saying he needed to do better and that they valued passion and creativity and long hours, his tweet was a peek into the leadership of an industry that still sees crunch time as a part of doing business. Sometimes they make the crunch time voluntary, but who is going to look at their boss and say "Naw, no thanks, I am going to go home" without fearing for their job?

SO WHY IS THIS LIKE A PORT CALL?

Similar to putting a bunch of Coasties on a ship for a few months and then letting them loose into port, crunch time has the effect of pushing people past their stress tolerances into headspaces that make them make risky and often stupid or even dangerous decisions. Note: I am not even going to touch the stories of sexual assault at conventions; that would be a whole book unto itself, but let me tell you it is very similar to what happens during a port call.

This isn't about the alcoholism that plagues both groups either. This is about the crunch.

Look, you can't not go out to sea when your job is literally protecting the ocean and the people on it. There will always be times when you need to be on a boat out in the middle of the ocean swearing if you don't see something other than an empty horizon soon, you are going to wear your shorts on your head, socks on your hands, and start running around the boat singing "Baby Shark." There will always be times at work where there is no other way ahead other than to put your head down and grind to get through something and get something done, those late crunchy hours.

But staying in a crunch or keeping your team in a state of constant crunch is not sustainable. Imagine if, when pulling in a ship, the Coast Guard told the crew, "Yeah, we know we are at the pier, but you can't leave the ship at all for the next three months because we just have a lot to get done." You are going to have problems.

CRUNCH IS FOR POTATO CHIPS

So how do you avoid being in the land of constant crunch? Prioritize, say no, and clearly communicate where you are at against a deadline. Most people fall down on the last two.

Prioritizing is likely something you have learned to do in some fashion since you started your career. Heck, even at your very first job, you likely learned at least a little about how to prioritize. If not, go back and read the chapter about asking questions. If you are feeling especially spicy, put things in perspective with the question, are you dying? Okay, then stop acting like it.

Saying no is, for a lot of people, one of the hardest things to do at work, for women especially because we have to battle against the perception of being a bitch or being difficult by saying no. You have to learn to say no in order to avoid driving your team toward collapsible burnout. Hell, as a leader, it is your job to teach and empower them to say no as well.

The most effective method for telling someone to go to hell—er, I mean no—isn't to do it with a smile but with clearly documented priorities. When you are making a new you have a list of MVP features—minimum viable product. Along the way, you are going to battle more hordes of good idea fairies than a semi-truck battles bugs on a summer highway. And like those bugs on a windshield, the good idea fairies can make a total mess of your project. Now, from time to time, hidden in with the good idea fairies is an actual sensible suggestion that could be worth pivoting for because of changing circumstances. You need to learn how to spot those.

For the rest, think about what you would drop down in priority from your current list in order to make this new thing happen. No, not simply add it to the list because the team could work an extra twenty hours this week because this is super cool, but what becomes a lesser priority? If there is nothing on the list you want to give less time to, then the new thing is not that important and can be backlogged.

Of course, there are certain times when you don't get a choice and you have to add that new Jenga block your dog found under the couch to the top of the already overbalanced tower. Well, shit, that sucks. Seriously look at how much this new thing is going to interrupt your schedule if you don't do the extra crunch time with it.

- Is it a reasonable amount of time, or is it adding three years?
- Will being late cause more damage to your brand/product than leaving this new thing out would?

The third point comes in here—clearly communicating. When your product that has been announced to the world is going to be late, you need to carefully balance when you tell the public. Told the wrong way and too soon, and presales drop, stock drops, or customers lose interest. Told too late, and the same can happen.

Interesting fact: I have never seen a game release delayed to take care of their people result in complete and utter meltdowns from anyone but trolls. So many companies enforce insane crunch lengths and still miss their launch date. Making the reaction even worse is when customers know you have abusive labor tactics, don't communicate you are going to be late early enough, and then are not only late but then the game also doesn't live up to hype.

Now you have exhausted people who gave up their lives for possible years to be a part of a project that has fans livid. Was it worth it?

You have to clearly communicate the expectations of delivery time to your teams, you need to clearly communicate your values and plans to your expectant customers, and you need to determine your priorities. You can have healthy, creative minds working away at making cool shit, or you can have exhausted people who can still make cool shit but burn out quickly. Know what really messes up your deadlines? Someone quitting right in the middle of a big project. Unlike on a ship where walking away from your job could leave you in the Mariana Trench, people can quit a company that is constantly crunched.

So basically, the lesson here is the Coast Guard taught me that you don't lock a bunch of people up on a giant metal dumpster in the ocean unless you have a good reason to have them out there. While crunch time at a gaming company means battling lines of code, bugs, and caffeine crashes, more so than battling the waves, people need more than a life ring in the form bag of Doritos or endless cold brew on tap to make it through crunch time. They need to know there is light at the end of the tunnel, they need to have a sustainable plan to get out of the crunch, and they need to know what you are going to do to try to avoid crunch in the future.

CHAPTER 14

Actually Give a Shit

"So, what do you do?" is a common question at the beginning of many conversations, especially in America. Equating the importance of people to the job they do is an irritating thing about our society. I am not talking about the importance as in this role of VP is more important than this janitor, though that exists too, but that a person themselves is only as valuable as the job or rank they have. That is utter bullshit. Just because someone is of a lower rank than you, or does a job that society has told you is of inherently "less value" than yours, does not mean that person is less worthy of respect or being treated like a person.

One thing I was never good at when I was an officer was maintaining that officer "bearing" when it came to the enlisted. I am not talking about fraternization; in fact, after my first tour, I did not drink more than a single drink at any work event, and I did not socialize with the majority of people I worked with outside of work. I rarely went to parties or other social events. This caused other problems, like me getting a reputation for being an "ice bitch" who couldn't relax, but I accepted that.

I am going to likely piss off a bunch of "leaders" with this next statement. A sad number of them are elitists who can't tell the difference between just being a person with an opinion or expertise and a breakdown in good order and discipline. I straight up had peers who didn't bother to say hi to a "nonrate"—even the term for them is awkward if we are being honest—or ask a third class petty officer how their day was, let alone ask for any sort of input from them. They had this attitude of superiority that made my teeth itch even though I knew the way officers are trained feeds into this attitude. Academy graduates were especially bad about this.

Yeah, that's right, I said it. Academy grads have a lot to be proud of. Getting into an Academy is brutal. I know, I got accepted in 1997 then chose to go to a civilian college anyway, if you recall. Getting through one is even harder. That being said, ask any enlisted member of any rank what they think of junior officers right out of the Academy and watch for the tell-tale twitch that goes with trying to hide a cringe as they find something noncommittal to say.

The Academy works hard to put a polish on their graduates, and that sometimes turns into a veneer of superiority that it takes time to get rid of. Some never get rid of it at all. That's not to say officer commissioned through other paths were always better; there were more than a few who took their shoulder pads to mean they were better than as well.

Of course, it is not *all* officers or Academy grads, and yes, I have plenty of Academy friends, but even they agreed with me on this particular issue. This can be seen based on the elitism of going to certain colleges. You also see this better than you veneer develop over time as someone gets higher in rank, from admiral to vice presidents. Don't act like you haven't met them.

YOUR PEOPLE ARE… PEOPLE

Here is where another piece of advice from my dad came into play. My dad was, in fact, an Academy grad, but he was the son of an enlisted Coastie, so he had a different perspective than many academy grads. He said, "You are only as successful as your people, and you can never forget that that is what they are first… people."

The same difference I saw between officers and enlisted is what I have seen between a lot of executives and non-executives in the corporate world. While, yes, there is a level of celebrity that comes with being a high-level executive at certain places, such as AWS, it doesn't change how you put your pants on in the morning. Or that sometimes your dog gets sick and you can't focus on your job that day. Or that you feel like no one listens to you. Or you wonder if people think you know what you are doing. The worries you have might change, in size or scope, when you get promoted, but the human condition doesn't.

To that end, I have never understood leaders who rule like dictators.

GIVE SPACE FOR VOICES

One of the things I always appreciated about Andy Jassy when I was at AWS was if you were in the room, you had a voice. It didn't matter that I was "just" an L6 in a room full of L10s; I had expertise and a voice.

When I was an L7 and the principle for the AWS Disaster Response team, this meant I felt comfortable—admittedly nervous—enough to write to him about the COVID-19 situation early in 2020, before most companies had begun shutting down. I knew from my conversations with different agencies that what we were seeing from our field teams, and my disaster background, this was going to be bad, and I felt a responsibility to say something.

Had I not worked in an environment where I knew I could email our CEO directly with a concern that big without being punished, my concerns would have likely been caught up in the email game of hoping the next person up the chain didn't think I was being overly paranoid until it got to him. In a situation like that, those sort of red tape delays can literally cost someone their life.

The leader who wants to hear all the voices in the room is the kind of leader I have always aimed to emulate; a leader who is willing to change their mind if the right data is presented.

I spent some time talking to Ariel Kelman, CMO of Salesforce, about empathetic leadership. Having worked with him at AWS, he is one of my top three leaders I have ever worked for, largely because of his people skills. Not to say he didn't sometimes put me in my place, but even when I had made a mistake or was confused about something, he never made me feel less than. In meetings, he welcomed opinions from everyone, no matter their rank.

Funny story: the first time I met Ariel was when I was walking off the elevator before my first re:Invent, wearing a shirt that said "Not enough coffee or middle fingers for today." When I almost ran into him—because of course I wasn't paying attention to where I was going—he read my shirt. In that split second before he reacted, my brain had enough time to have a "junior officer just did something stupid in front of the new admiral, oh god, I am in so much trouble" melt down. His laugh and "Like the shirt" as he got into the elevator immediately stopped that noise. It also humanized a leader who, until that point, I had only seen during large meetings.

When I told Ariel he was one of the most empathetic high EQ people I had ever worked for, he chuckled. He told me he couldn't understand why it was so hard for other leaders to recognize that people are what make the team.

I went on to tell him the story of a young woman who had worked for me at Oracle after he had departed, how she had told me she would never forget that in a meeting she had spoken up about an issue. She was so nervous saying anything as the most junior person in the room, and others in the meeting messaged her asking what she was doing, but Ariel listened and engaged with her. Not only did he do so without judgment, he really heard her and made her feel valued. To this young woman, that meant everything.

When I relayed this story, he replied that while he remembered that meeting, he hadn't realized it would have meant so much to the young woman, because to him, everyone in the room has a reason for being there and brings something to the table.

"It just makes good business sense," he explained to me when I mentioned that, in my experience, a leader who wants to hear from everyone in the room no matter how junior wasn't the norm. It was that simple. Being a leader who listens to their people and sees them as people just makes good business sense.

At the end of the day, you need to remember that your people are just that—people. They have hopes and dreams, and they are playing a game all their own. Just because someone has been at a level for years without moving up doesn't mean they aren't successful. This one is especially hard for military members who lived in an up or out environment. It could likely mean they have other life goals or they are working on a different timeline than you.

Remember

- Listen to your people. People were hired to your team for a reason.
- Be humble enough to change your mind.
- Help your team grow and shine, and you will shine too.
- Just because you wear the shoulder boards doesn't mean you have more value than the people who work for you. You have more responsibility.
- Power without empathy makes you an asshole.

Now that we have talked about how you look out for your people and embracing who they are, I should point out it is just as important to look out for yourself. This means both covering your ass and documenting your wins, and it is easier than you might think.

CHAPTER 15

Promotion Fodder... er Folders

Your boss probably can't tell you beyond a broad scope what you did in the last year. More than likely, once you accomplished your goals, the accomplishment dripped from their brain like pour-over through a Chemex. Sure, it was important for the pot of Sunday morning coffee, but the details are lost in the mix. Your boss also doesn't know you reminded that guy over on the product team three times of an upcoming deadline he still missed and now your project is going to be late.

This is why you need to keep a junk drawer of your accomplishments and a Steve folder for covering your ass. Let me explain.

Every year in the Coast Guard, officers have an Officer Evaluation Report. Think of this as a corporate annual evaluation's mean-as-fuck cousin that not only wants to talk about how you did your job but your weight, your writing capabilities, how you wear your clothes, and a whole host of other things.

ATTACHMENTS:

3. PERFORMANCE OF DUTIES: Measures an officer's ability to manage and to get things done.

Category	1	3	5	7	N/O
a. PLANNING AND PREPAREDNESS: Ability to anticipate, determine goals, identify relevant information, set priorities and deadlines, and create a shared vision of the unit's and Coast Guard's future.	Got caught by the unexpected; appeared to be controlled by events. Set vague or unrealistic goals. Used unreasonable criteria to set priorities and deadlines. Rarely had plan of action. Failed to focus on relevant information.	Consistently prepared. Set high but realistic goals. Used sound criteria to set priorities and deadlines. Used quality tools and processes to develop action plans. Identified key information. Kept supervisors and stake-holders informed.	Exceptional preparation. Always looked beyond immediate events or problems. Skillfully balanced competing demands. Developed strategies with contingency plans. Assessed all aspects of problems, including underlying issues and impact.		
b. USING RESOURCES: Ability to manage time, materials, information, money, and people (i.e. all CG components as well as external publics).	Concentrated on unproductive activities or often overlooked critical demands. Failed to use people productively. Did not follow up. Mismanaged information, money or time. Used ineffective tools or left subordinates without means to accomplish tasks. Employed wasteful methods.	Effectively managed a variety of activities with available resources. Delegated, empowered, and followed up. Skilled time manager, budgeted own and subordinates' time productively. Ensured subordinates had adequate tools, materials, time and direction. Cost conscious, sought ways to cut waste.	Unusually skilled at bringing scarce resources to bear on the most critical of competing demands. Optimized productivity through effective delegation, empowerment, and follow-up control. Found ways to systematically reduce cost, eliminate waste, and improve efficiency.		
c. RESULTS/EFFECTIVENESS: Quality, quantity, timeliness and impact of work.	Routine tasks accomplished with difficulty. Results often late or of poor quality. Work had a negative impact on department or unit. Maintained the status quo despite opportunities to improve.	Got the job done in all routine situations and in many unusual ones. Work was timely and of high quality; required same of subordinates. Results had a positive impact on department or unit. Continuously improved services and organizational effectiveness.	Maintained optimal balance among quality, quantity, and timeliness of work. Quality of own and subordinates' work surpassed expectations. Results had a significant positive impact on unit or Coast Guard. Established clearly effective systems of continuous improvement.		
d. ADAPTABILITY: Ability to modify work methods and priorities in response to new information, changing conditions, political realities, or unexpected obstacles.	Unable to gauge effectiveness of work, recognize political realities, or make adjustments when needed. Overlooked or screened out new information. Overreacted or responded slowly to change in direction or environment. Ineffective in ambiguous, complex, or pressured situations.	Receptive to change, new information, and technology. Effectively used benchmarks to improve performance and service. Monitored progress and changed course as required. Effectively dealt with pressure and ambiguity. Facilitated smooth transitions. Adjusted direction to accommodate societal trends or political realities.	Rapidly assessed and adjusted to changing conditions, political realities, new information and technology. Very skilled at using and responding to measurement indicators. Championed organizational improvements. Effectively dealt with extremely complex situations. Turned pressure and ambiguity into constructive forces for change.		
e. PROFESSIONAL COMPETENCE: Ability to acquire, apply and share technical and administrative knowledge and skills associated with description of duties. (Includes operational aspects such as marine safety, seamanship, airmanship, SAR, etc., as appropriate.)	Questionable competence and credibility. Operational or specialty expertise inadequate or lacking in key areas. Made little effort to grow professionally. Used knowledge as power against others or bluffed rather than acknowledging ignorance. Effectiveness reduced due to limited knowledge of own organizational role and customer needs.	Competent and credible authority on specialty or operational issues. Acquired and applied excellent operational or specialty expertise for assigned duties. Showed professional growth through education, training and professional reading. Shared knowledge and information with others clearly and simply. Understood own organizational role and customer needs.	Superior expertise; advice and actions showed great breadth and depth of knowledge. Remarkable grasp of complex issues, concepts, and situations. Rapidly developed professional growth beyond expectations. Vigorously conveyed knowledge, directly resulting in increased workplace productivity. Insightful knowledge of own role, customer needs, and value of work.		

8. PERSONAL AND PROFESSIONAL QUALITIES: Measures selected qualities which illustrate the individual's character.					
	1	3	5	7	N/O
a. INITIATIVE: Ability to originate and act on new ideas, pursue opportunities to learn and develop, and seek responsibility without guidance and supervision.	Postponed needed action. Implemented or supported improvements only when directed to do so. Showed little interest in career development. Feasible improvements in methods, services, or products went unexplored.	Championed improvement through new ideas, methods, and practices; self-starter. Anticipated problems and took prompt action to avoid or resolve them. Sought opportunities for own career development. Pursued productivity gains and enhanced mission performance by applying new ideas and methods.	Aggressively sought out additional responsibility. A self-learner. Made worthwhile ideas and practices work when others might have given up. Extremely innovative. Optimized use of new ideas and methods to improve work processes, decision-making, and service delivery.		
b. JUDGMENT: Ability to make sound decisions and provide valid recommendations by using facts, experience, political acumen, common sense, risk assessment, and analytical thought.	Decisions often displayed poor analysis. Failed to make necessary decisions, or jumped to conclusions without considering facts, alternatives, and impact. Did not effectively weigh risk, cost, and time considerations. Unconcerned with political drivers on organization.	Demonstrated analytical thought and common sense in making decisions. Used facts, data, and experience, and considered the impact of alternatives and political realities. Weighed risk, cost and time considerations. Made sound decisions promptly with the best available information.	Combined keen analytical thought, an understanding of political processes, and insight to make appropriate decisions. Focused on the key issues and the most relevant information. Did the right thing at the right time. Actions indicated awareness of impact of decisions on others. Not afraid to take reasonable risks to achieve positive results.		
c. RESPONSIBILITY: Ability to act ethically, courageously, and dependably and inspire the same in others; accountability for own and subordinates' actions.	Actions demonstrated questionable ethics or lack of commitment. Tolerated indifference or failed to hold subordinates accountable. Allowed organization to absorb personnel problems rather than confronting them as required. Tended not to speak up or get involved. Provided minimal support for decisions counter to own ideas.	Held self and subordinates personally and professionally accountable. Spoke up when necessary, even when expressing unpopular positions. Supported organizational policies and decisions which may have been counter to own ideas. Committed to the successful achievement of organizational goals.	Integrity and ethics beyond reproach. Always held self and subordinates to highest standards of personal and professional accountability. Did the right thing even when it was difficult. Succeeded in making even unpopular policies or decisions work. Actions demonstrated unwavering commitment to achievement of organizational goals.		
d. PROFESSIONAL PRESENCE: Ability to bring credit to the Coast Guard through one's actions, competence, demeanor, and appearance. Extent to which an officer displayed the Coast Guard's core values of honor, respect, and devotion to duty.	Unaware of general CG objectives; uncooperative or biased in interactions. Lost composure in difficult situations. Conveyed poor image of self and CG. Ignorant of or sloppy with common military courtesies. Uniform appearance and grooming below standard. Failed to display the core values of honor, respect, and devotion to duty.	Knowledgeable in how CG objectives serve the public; cooperative and fair in all interactions. Composed in difficult situations. Conveyed positive image of self and CG. Well versed in military etiquette; precise in rendering and upholding military courtesies. Great care in uniform appearance and grooming. Abided by the core values of honor, respect, and devotion to duty.	Always self-assured, projected ideal CG image. Poised in response to others' provocative actions. Contributed leadership role in civilian/military community. Exemplified and held others accountable for the core values and finest traditions of military customs and protocol. Meticulous uniform appearance and grooming; inspired similar standards in others.		
e. HEALTH AND WELL-BEING: Ability to invest in the Coast Guard's future by caring for the physical health, safety, and emotional well-being of self and others.	Did not adhere to the Coast Guard Fitness Program. Failed to meet minimum standards of weight control or sobriety. Tolerated or condoned others' alcohol abuse. Seldom considered subordinates' health and well-being. Unwilling or unable to recognize and manage stress despite apparent need. Failed to adequately identify and protect personnel from safety hazards.	Maintained weight standards and adhered to the Coast Guard Fitness Program. Committed to health and well-being of self and subordinates. Enhanced personal performance through activities supporting physical and emotional well-being. Recognized and managed stress effectively. Ensured that safe operating procedures were followed.	Remarkable vitality, enthusiasm, alertness and energy. Consistently contributed at high levels and actively followed a comprehensive fitness program. Optimized personal performance through involvement in activities which supported physical and emotional well-being. Monitored and helped others deal with stress, enhance health and well-being. Demonstrated a significant commitment towards safety of personnel.		

That's right, once a year, you needed to compile not only every job-related accomplishment but also anything else that might be able to prove to a board sometime in the future you were worth retaining. Up or out is the way of the service, meaning even if you are a high performer, if you don't make the cut for some reason, you don't just get to stick around; you have to leave the service.

That's what happened to me, even after all the groundbreaking things I had done for the service, and the fact they had educated me to the point they couldn't afford to hire someone with my expertise, I got passed over and had to get out of the service. Unlike many of my peers, I actually wasn't bothered by this; I was excited. Remember, play the game the way you need to to get to your win state.

As I type this, I make more than an admiral and get to decide on my own what pants I wear every day.

THE PROCESS

In the United States Coast Guard, officer evaluations are a formal process used to assess and document the performance and potential of Coast Guard officers. These evaluations play a crucial role in determining career progression, promotions, and assignments within the organization.

The Coast Guard uses a system called the Officer Evaluation System (OES) to conduct these assessments. Here is how it is *supposed* to work. It is up for debate if this system is effective or too subjective, but it does provide a good lesson here.

1. Evaluation Period: The evaluation period usually covers one year, beginning on July 1 and ending on June 30 of the following year. During this time, officers are observed and evaluated on their performance, leadership abilities, adherence to core values, and other relevant factors.

2. Supervisor Input: The immediate supervisors of the officer, such as commanding officers or department heads, provide input and assessments based on their observations and interactions with the officer. They assess the officer's strengths, weaknesses, and overall performance. As you can imagine, the amount of effort put in, as well as evaluation criteria, can vary wildly depending on the manager.

3. Self-Assessment: Officers are typically required to complete a self-assessment, where they reflect on their own performance, accomplishments, and areas for improvement. This self-assessment provides an opportunity for officers to provide their perspectives and contribute to the evaluation process. This is actually where the majority of the writing of the OER is done.

4. Evaluation Form: The evaluations are documented using the Coast Guard Officer Evaluation Report (OER) form. See diagram for an example.

5. Review and Endorsement: The completed evaluation report goes through a review process, and not dissimilar to in the civilian world, they are reviewed up the leadership chain.

The evaluation report assigns performance marks to the officer, typically ranging from one (poor) to seven (outstanding). Basically, "You need to be kicked out of the service because you suck" to "holy crap, this officer might be able to walk on water," in the category they got a seven in at least. Then, on the last page, there is an area where your boss fills out if they think you should be promoted, and where they think you stand in regards to your peer.

You think companies like Microsoft stack rank? Imagine for a moment that you are being compared to everyone at your level, no matter what their skill set is. Engineer? Yep. Marketer? Yeah, them too. Oh, a Lawyer? Yep, they are in there right alongside a software developer in the same system.

As you can imagine, OERs are pretty stressful things for officers, and you learn right out of training that you cannot rely on your superior officer—aka manager—to be tracking your efforts to the level of detail needed for the document. No joke, in OCS, I had a staff officer tell me to carefully document everything I did every week.

The Venn diagram of people who were OER "bullet hounds"—you know, the ones you could tell were only doing things for the OER and wrote down everything they did like they were the second coming of Alexander Hamilton— and the people who would step on you to get ahead? It is a circle.

Here's the problem. I have ADHD—though I was not diagnosed at the time—and the thought of sitting every week to create a bulleted list sounded like my personal hell.

DIGITAL JUNK DRAWER

The point at the core of the "write it all down all the time"
makes sense though. You should not rely on anyone other
than yourself to keep track of your accomplishments. I have
found a method that works better for not only myself but
has worked well for my teams. Basically, a digital—and often
a physical—notebook of wins. On my desktop at all times,
there is a file called YAY, and there is always a file called
Steve. I'll explain Steve in a bit.

This folder idea, as it turns out, has a name in the ADHD
world it is called a doom box, the place for the odds and ends
you can't throw away but don't really know how to sort. Then,
when you need some weird thing, say the metal needle for
inflating basketballs, you know where to go to find it.

Listen, when you accomplish a small task your boss asked
you to do, it might not mean much to you in the moment,
and you don't know if you should hold on to it or not. You
put it in your YAY folder, because you might find out in a
few weeks the small task you did was a part of a bigger effort
that led to something amazing. Or maybe one small task is
something that, over the course of the year, you have done
enough variations of to have accomplished a larger goal, or
to have an impressive overall picture when you put all the
smaller pieces together.

Create a similar folder in your email inbox for the same
kind of files—the emails talking about a completed project,
or even better, kudos you get from your leadership or peers.
This second one, the kudos, serves two purposes. One, it
can help you when you are sitting down and trying to figure

out how to show your impact to try for a promotion. Two, in the really shitty days, you can go into your folder and get nice little dopamine hits by reading over the times someone thanked you for being awesome.

EVALUATION TIME

Now that you have set up your YAY folder and your annual self-evaluation has come around, there you sit staring at the folder and a blinking cursor. One more tool can get you from the folder to a great evaluation. Invest in a performance phrases book. Yes, like a physical one, one you can flip pages in. One you can close your eyes, turn to a random page, put your finger on it, open your eyes, and use as the starting phrase to one of your value statements.

Look, I am sure someone is going to read this and say, "Well, can't ChatGPT write my performance evaluations?" I am sure you could do it that way, but by the time you are done putting in the specifics to get the thing finely tuned to you as a person, or one of your people, you likely could have just written the entire thing yourself with the help of a handy performance phrase guide.

That's it, there you have it. This is the way I have gotten myself and others around me promoted with an almost perfect success rate. Like many, I am better at getting others promoted than myself.

1. Create a YAY folder on your desktop and in your inbox.
2. Throw in those folders all your finished projects or kudos emails.

3. Get a performance phrasebook.
4. Sit down when it is time to write up the performance review and look at the categories you need to talk about.
5. Now sort your junk drawer, go through those YAY folders to find projects or emails to start building your story.
6. Use a performance phrase book to help you find creative ways to say positive "Look at what I accomplished" shit in new and creative ways.

Along with the YAY folder, it is important to talk about having your Steve folder. My apologies in advance to the Steves of the world.

SORRY, NOT SORRY, STEVE

When I started at AWS, I had a coworker, Steve, I just couldn't seem to communicate with. No matter what I did, the emails came back in an abrasive tone, and we spiraled. I started collecting all of his emails into a folder labeled Steve because his emails tended to piss me off so badly I didn't even want to see them sitting staring at me in my inbox. Frankly, they were infuriating to the point that I went to my boss and told him if they didn't do something about Steve, I wanted someone else to take on the project or I was going to do something drastic.

Instead, my boss sat me and Steve down and had us talk. Not about work, but about the fact we were both into tabletop games, which led to a bunch of other conversations, which eventually led to a professional friendship I still count as valuable today. It turned out, Steve just didn't come across well in emails, and from that time on, whenever he was drafting something where he was frustrated, I actually became the person he would send the draft to so I could help him sort the subtext. He became my staunch ally in many projects that ruffled a lot of feathers.

One day, I realized even though Steve and I were no longer adversarial, I had not changed the name of the Steve folder. I still used it, for CYA kind of emails. You know, the email with someone being a bit over-the-top rude, or dropping the ball on something, or email copies of emails I had sent that I knew I would need for a paper trail later. They all went in the Steve folder.

When I told Steve about this folder, he burst out laughing. Not only did it not bother him I still had it labeled the Steve folder, he told me to leave it labeled as a reminder that not everyone who ended up in there was irredeemable or impossible to work with; they just might take a little more effort.

CYA WITH STEVE

The CYA, or Steve, folder is also something the Coast Guard inadvertently taught me to do: always have the documentation and a paper trail to protect you in case something goes wrong. For example, at one tour of duty, I had just returned from disaster response, and less than two weeks later, there was an operational inspection for the command center I was in, which included a written test.

I had been gone more than sixty days, which meant I was no longer qualified to stand watch and would have to requalify. I wrote to the junior officer—my peer—to ask them if I would need to take the test since it was for qualified Command Duty Officers (CDOs) and I wouldn't be one until I was requalified. I was told in writing in response that no, I was not going to take the test due to my needing to requalify.

Imagine my surprise in the grocery store a few days later when I got a phone call from the officer in charge of the command center asking where the hell I was and what I thought I was doing skipping out on the test. I quickly left the grocery store and hauled ass to the command center, where my superior officer would hear none of [my] excuses, and I needed to sit down to take the test immediately. It was the first time in my life I completely and utterly failed a test—like not even remotely close to passing utterly failed the test. My peers had been studying for it for weeks; I was thrown into it cold after being told I didn't have to take it.

So, armed with the email from my peer who was supposed to be coordinating the inspection, along with the documents showing I was not supposed to have been taking the test as I needed to requalify for my position, I went to the command. I was able to show my test score should not be used against the overall command center score and, in fact, should be thrown out entirely. I went back to the process of requalifying for my role and had to take the test the following round when it came up again. Weirdly enough, when I knew there was a test coming, I passed with flying colors.

KEEP THOSE RECEIPTS

That situation was not the first time I had found keeping a concise paper trail—and knowing the rules—to be critical to my success, and to this day, I keep a Steve folder, and often project-specific folders, of anything that might be critical in the future for analysis or simply covering my team's ass when someone tries to throw us under the bus.

Unlike the YAY folder and evaluation process, the Steve folder process is easy.

- Create a Steve folder in your inbox. Call it whatever you like.
- Put emails with conflict or issues, or documentation into the Steve folder.
- Hope you never need to open the folder.
- If you do, welp. Bombs away.

When I have talked to my teams about these folders, the interesting thing I have found is most everyone has a Steve folder, or some way of covering their ass setup, but way fewer people had a wins folder. This might be because of what psychologists call the negativity bias the majority of humans have, where we as a species focus on the negative outcomes as a survival mechanism.

Studies have also shown negative information tends to influence evaluations more strongly than comparably extreme positive information,[1] which makes it even more important to have a YAY folder ready to remind your boss how kick ass you are after you maybe messed something up the week before annual evaluations.

So what do you do when your Steve folder is overflowing and your YAY folder looks like Death Valley after Burning Man? It might be time for you to start thinking about saying fuck it.

CHAPTER 16

Everything is a Crisis

If everything is a crisis then nothing is a crisis. You have probably heard some variation of this, where the basic meaning is there is someone at work who treats everything like a huge dramatic fire, resulting in absolutely nothing being an actual fire. Let's call them the Chicken Littles of the office; the sky is constantly falling and they need everyone to know, and they need everyone to be all hands on deck all the time to make whatever it is work.

Frankly, it's exhausting.

Now, one of my jobs in the Coast Guard was search and rescue operations, and the other? Crisis communications for things like hurricanes, homicides, bridge collapses, plane crashes, the list goes on. You know what causes a serious case of side eye for those Chicken Littles of the office world? The things I have done in my career.

To quote my friend and "big brother" CDR Chris O'Neil, USCG retired, "But did you die?"

He liked to use this quippy little one-liner any time we faced adversity or a major problem. Did you die? Nope? Okay good, pull on your boots, suck it up, and let's go. This chapter isn't about telling you to suck it up; in fact, in the next chapter, you will find I am not a huge fan of the embrace the suck bullshit mentality. What is important to understand for this chapter is when I say I have been through real crises, I am talking about killer Hurricanes, major oil spills, and a global pandemic, in a response capacity.

PERSPECTIVE IS EVERYTHING

My version of what constitutes a crisis, thanks to the Coast Guard, is likely different than your average manager. This means while I do get stressed out, I generally have a higher threshold for becoming panicked or losing my shit. The same is likely true for most veterans you work with.

Ready for the secret? If you plan for anything to turn into a crisis, the likelihood it will become a crisis lessens. Even better, if you plan this way and someone does go off the rails, you are ready because you have done your dressing drills.

Wait hold on, you say. You just made fun of Chicken Littles, and now you are telling me to be one. Nope. Buzzer sound. What I am telling you is to approach each project as though it were a crisis, or has the potential to become one. Take that natural anxiety you have and make it a superpower.

When the shit hits the fan, from typhoons to train derailments, responders use a system called the Incident Command System (ICS). This structured framework is not merely a protocol; it's the compass that guides responders through the storm of emergencies, transforming chaos into control through a system both structured and flexible at once. Whole books have been written on it, and there are more classes to train you on it than there are mantis shrimp in the sea, but here is a quick breakdown of what it is.

The Incident Command System (ICS) was initially developed to address the complexities of firefighting operations and has evolved into a versatile framework applicable to various scenarios, from natural disasters to public health crises. At its heart lies a simple concept: unity of command.

Like a symphony conductor who leads a diverse ensemble of instruments to create harmony, the ICS unites various agencies and personnel under a single chain of command. It doesn't matter where the person comes from, be it from the Coast Guard, the local fire department, or National Fish and Wildlife, they all have their roles in the unified command, where experience tops rank and people all know how to speak the same jargon. This ensures everyone dances to the same tune, preventing the chaotic cacophony that would arise if everyone played their own notes. Looking at you, FEMA.

Within the ICS, there's a careful choreography of roles and responsibilities. Just as a theater troupe seamlessly transitions from scene to scene, ICS designates specific functions to specialized units that transition from stage to stage of the response. ICS operates on a hierarchical structure designed to foster clear lines of authority; let me tell you, people in tech loathe this, the idea of a hierarchy of command.

At its nucleus, the incident commander assumes the central role, possessing overall responsibility for strategic decision-making. Surrounding this pivotal figure, the organization expands into distinct sections including operations, planning, logistics, and finance/administration. Each section is bestowed with specific responsibilities, ensuring the multifaceted aspects of an incident are systematically addressed.

The span of control dictates supervisors oversee a manageable number of subordinates, maintaining clear lines of communication and promoting effective delegation. Moreover, the flexibility of the ICS enables seamless integration with various agencies and organizations, thereby promoting interagency collaboration and cross-functional expertise.

Imagine a wildfire spreading its fiery fingers across the landscape. The ICS becomes a sentinel amidst the inferno, strategizing and adapting. The planning section crafts a battle plan, using terrain and weather like chess pieces. The operations section rallies firefighters and resources to execute the plan, each move a calculated step toward victory. Meanwhile, logistics ensures the warriors are well fed and well armed, supplying them as if preparing for a grand medieval quest.

A defining characteristic of the ICS is its emphasis on communication as a keystone of effective emergency management. The use of standard terminology and clear channels of communication ensures information is disseminated accurately and promptly, under a clearly established cadence. The incident briefing facilitates the exchange of critical information among key personnel, enabling them to collectively form strategies and make informed decisions and then set timelines for taking action on the plan before coming back to check in on how the plan has gone.

Like I said, there are books and courses on this, so this is a brief summary. Why am I telling you this? Well, when you eat, sleep, and breathe ICS for most of your career, you naturally start applying it to everything else. When you add a healthy dose of ADHD and anxiety that makes you naturally look for every single way something could go wrong and you could be embarrassed or fuck something up, you either curl into a ball and give up or you make that shit into a superpower and get on with things.

TAKE A DEEP BREATH

Now, I am not saying you should go get yourself a huge dose of rampant anxiety, but I am saying the ICS system has some great lessons for you to build your project or team that can help you either prevent a shitstorm from happening or help you navigate it when it does.

First, make sure there are clear roles and responsibilities, even if you are not the one in charge. This can mean asking whoever is in charge to outline them and then if that person is a manager type who either doesn't know how to set lanes—Narwhals, usually—or leaves it up to you and your peers to sort it out—usually Seagulls—then you are going to need to talk with your peers and find out who is going to take on what.

As always, follow shit up in writing. Do not expect everyone in the group is going to remember what you talked about at the beginning or as the project changes or new shiny objects come up. Putting everything in writing is key throughout all of this to have a clear line of communication and understanding.

Now that you have established roles for the project or program, figure out your backups. As discussed in the redundancy chapter, backups are critical because people have lives and shit happens.

Once you have your structure ready, make sure teams outside your own know who they interface with for various asks. Don't go asking the operations person about stuff the logistics person should be handling and that sort of thing. People are going to mess it up and go to the person on your team they know, so your people need to be empowered to redirect asks to the appropriate team member. You really don't want your flight ops boss writing your press releases and so forth.

Make it clear how communications are going to work for your team. For example, when I was running the launch for the big event of the year, I started my meetings about the event seven months before. They were brief, they were simple, and they were just about getting everyone's brains in gear for what was coming. The closer we got to the event, the simpler I kept communications, but I made them more frequent. For a lot of you, this might mean using the Agile model of stand ups or some other scrummy thing. No matter what the cadence, make it clear, documented, and understood.

Beyond the meeting cadence, we established, for blog posts, you had to turn in a ticket and all communications about the blog post would happen either in the ticket or the draft of the post itself. We did this to minimize the confusion from back and forth emails or instant messages where people got dropped from threads or side conversations were happening. There is a reason why the Blog Team had hoodies that said in big bold letters across the back "Is it in the ticket?"

In the tangled mess that is office communications, it's like we opened a box of crayons and threw them at a wall to see what stuck. Fun fact, crayons don't stick. Emails fly all over like digital paper airplanes passing in the night, Slack messages ping pong at the speed of a caffeinated chihuahua, and don't get me started on team forums. It's like a game of telephone where someone says, "Let's get burgers for lunch," and by the time it gets to the whole team, it's some sort of proposal for a hamster powered commuter train. With so many different digital channels to use for communication, is it any surprise the grapevine is now growing watermelons? You have to get that shit on lock.

FITS ALL SIZES

This isn't just for running big events though. Set up your team this way, where everyone is speaking the same jargon, and if someone is new, have someone teach them. Don't expect the new kid to get what the heck the acronyms are; give them the right resources.

Once you have established the lanes and the communications set up, use the brain trust that is the team to look for any issues coming over the horizon. This can be really hard to do since we all get caught up in the day-to-day, but a part of making sure you look for a crisis before it can become one is to, well, look.

In order for this part to work, you are going to have built the trust with your team that speaking up when there is an issue does not come with any punishment or ridicule. Sometimes speaking up is the hardest thing a person can do, and if you want to avoid running aground, you need to have people who feel empowered to open their mouths and shout "Oh shit, rocks ahead!" before your ship runs aground.

There you have it. You can literally help prevent and be prepared for crisis by using the tools first responders do to respond to a crisis.

- Clearly establish roles. Check out the ICS structure below.
- Set up a communications cadence.
- Have clear communication pathways.
- Empower your people to speak up.

Then again, there are companies that act like everything is a crisis no matter how well you plan. Places where, due to bad leadership, a blue falcon, or just inexperience, you can't work around the issues and it is killing you.

I am not being hyperbolic there. Studies have shown stress at work can have serious impacts on your health. In fact, the long-term effects of stress include Cardiovascular disease, musculoskeletal disorders, and more.[1]

INCIDENT ORGANIZATION CHART (ICS 207)

1. Incident Name:

2. Operational Period: Date From: Date To:
Time From: Time To:

3. Organization Chart

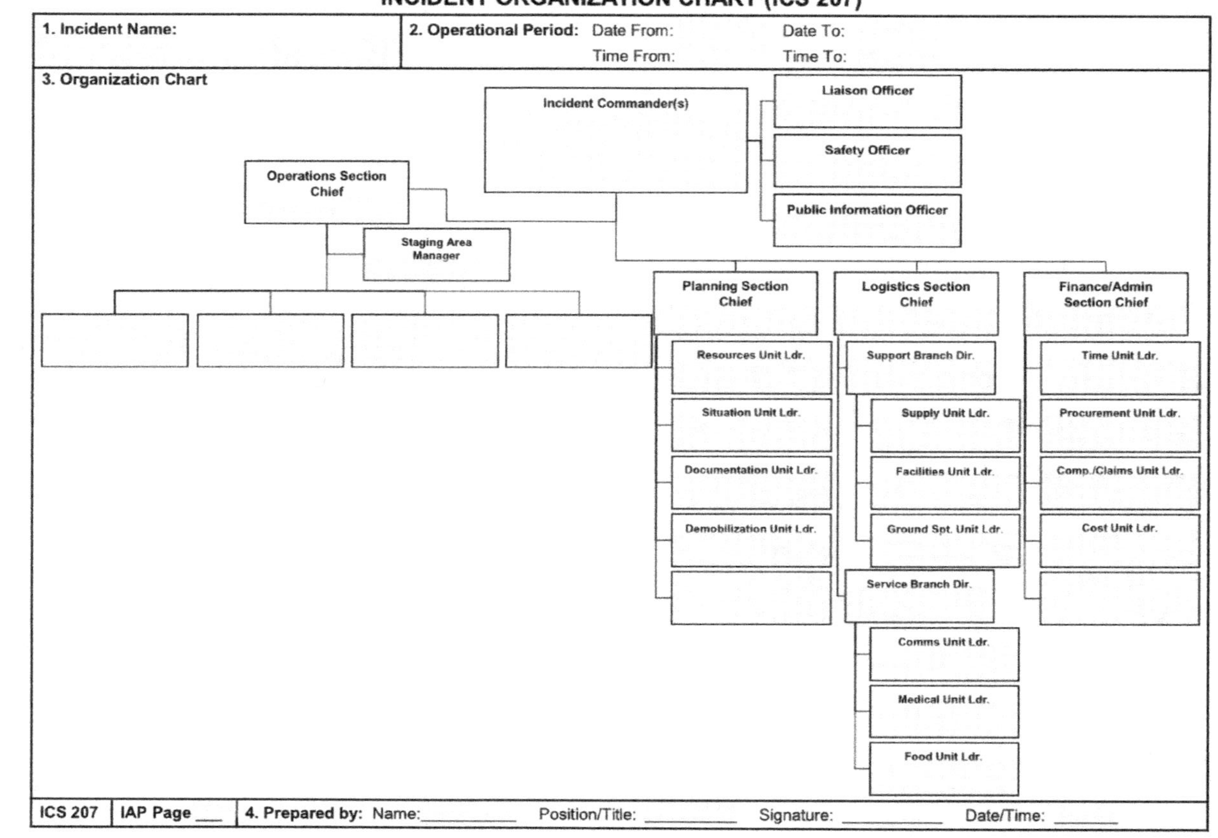

ICS 207 | **IAP Page** ___ | **4. Prepared by:** Name:__________ Position/Title: _________ Signature: __________ Date/Time: ________

So what do you do if you are in that situation? What do you do when you have simply had it with the fire drills or toxicity? Would you be surprised if my answer was... fuck it? Seriously, fuck it. For two such simple words, it is never quite that simple a decision.

CHAPTER 17

F*ck It, Quit

Some people you know you'll miss when they are gone, but there are some people you cannot fathom life without. The thought of losing them doesn't hurt you like you think it "should" because your mind simply cannot think past the infinite depths you would fall to if they weren't in the world anymore. I felt like that about Kate.

I know this is a dramatic way to head into the end of this book, especially with how snarky I have been up until this point. All that said, this is important, so bear with me.

If there are soulmates in the world, I'd like to think they can also come in the shape of a best friend. Someone who doesn't just love the good and the bad but knows the mistakes, the mortifying straight-up fuck-ups you have had, and says *I got you*; someone who lets you know you don't have to keep setting yourself on fire to keep others warm—then offers to light them on fire to keep you warm instead. That was my Kate.

As I tugged on the stupid red ringmaster jacket I had found on Amazon and bought for this exact moment, she would have been looking at me with a smirk. She would have thought—and probably said—as she watched me adjust the overpriced absurdity of a lace-trimmed top hat, that I was utterly ridiculous. I always think of her when I am at my most fragile, especially in moments where I am scared and the imposter syndrome is creeping in.

Kate, who I lost in a hiking accident in May of 2017, would have also told me to get my shit together. She'd get that wicked grin of hers and tell me to go in there, blow their minds, and fuck everyone who ever said I couldn't do yet another "impossible" thing.

She'd also tell me right now to focus and get on with the story.

I shook myself off, squaring my shoulders against the less than six hours sleep I managed to steal in the last two days. I pushed open the door at 5:00 a.m. in Las Vegas and walked across a ballroom that held about one hundred exhausted people. We had been running through coffee at a rate of ten gallons per day, the upbeat playlists providing water wings to our drowning brains. Caffeine and Taylor Swift can only do so much, and people were close to breaking or saying fuck it and walking out.

I snagged a conference chair near the end of the room, praying it was sturdy enough and that my black riding boots wouldn't slip. As I took a deep breath of that Vegas Strip air, inhaling more recycled air than a TIE fighter pilot in *Return of the Jedi*, I was glad I hadn't eaten yet that morning. I was regretting starting in on that ten gallons of coffee already. I threw my arms out wide with a big show smile, and in a voice built from years of singing, theatre, and a dash of military command voice, announced, "Good morning!"

My projected voice would have done my Russian voice instructor proud. The room went silent, everyone knowing that if I had raised my voice to that level, I needed their attention. Ana talks a lot; she can be scary, but she never yells. Another deep breath and I continued.

"This is it. This is the biggest show of the week. You did it. You made it. Through the late nights, the crappy food, the stress… It has sucked, but here we are. This is what you have been working for. Today, you change the world. It might not be for some big company… It might be for some small developer in Wisconsin, who just might be the one to save hundreds of lives someday, or just make someone's life a little easier. So I know most of us are tired and over all this. Let's go change the world."

As I walked across the room to my team, who had been coordinating a hundred wizards behind one big curtain, they gave me a variety of looks; some had teary eyes, all wore smiles. As I sat, my team member who was an Army vet said wryly, "Really? A *Braveheart* moment?"

And the woman on my team who had known me since grad school said in the most goth dry tones, "Draaaaaaama."

In that moment, I went from struggling between keeping the "I got this mask" on or bursting into tears, to laughing with my team like we had all lost our minds. Honestly, by that point, I am pretty sure we had. Hey, at least the tears running down my cheeks were from laughing.

IN THE MOMENT

I suppose thinking of my dead best friend in such a corporate moment might sound dramatic, but don't we all think of the people who would have given us the advice and strength we need in moments to get through them? That's what the 2018 AWS re:Invent was for me. The Sisyphean task of launching more services and features than most tech companies launched in a year in four days. Sounds easy, right?

By numbers, it was more than one hundred and forty teams, but I couldn't tell you how many people that worked out to. For anyone not familiar with Amazon Web Services, if you are reading this on a Kindle, or listening to it as a book, if you bought it from a webpage, if you are about to go catch up on Netflix, if you are going to do some online shopping, you have used AWS services. The OG cloud provider, Wikipedia defines AWS as Amazon Web Services, Inc. AWS is a subsidiary of Amazon that provides on-demand cloud computing platforms and APIs to individuals, companies, and governments, on a metered, pay-as-you-go basis.

AWS re:Invent was the company's annual conference, arguably the largest cloud computing conference in the world with approximately seventy-five thousand people. Ah, the innocent days of ignorant bliss that was pre-COVID-19. During that week, while attendees wandered the show floor and bounced between sessions like a vaguely demented Disneyland—looking at you, re:Play party—there was an entire team of characters behind the scenes making the magic happen.

That year, I wasn't only one of the characters; I was the chaos coordinator. Oh, who I am kidding, I was the ringmaster of the shit show. I just had to make it through Andy Jassy's—AWS CEO at the time—keynote and I could rest. I could go to my hotel room and cry until I threw up. I mean, it wouldn't be the first time in the last four months that had happened. The only difference now would be the hotel had a way nicer bathtub than I did at home.

Nice bathtubs aside, AWS re:invent was hell. You can ask anyone who has worked on a product launch for AWS re: Invent, or a keynote, or running the blog platform. That's what I did my first year at the event in 2016: I ran one blog helping the VP of Evangelism Jeff Barr publish blog posts for every major launch. The event took insane amounts of coordination, collaboration, and just straight up manic drive from everyone involved.

To be honest, of all the disasters that had gotten me to this point—not only from running the blog to running the show in two years—but what got me from being a kid who quit the

US Coast Guard Academy, moved to Antarctica, became an officer in the Coast Guard anyway, changed the very service itself, to being an executive at the third largest software company in the world? My willingness to be different, to step outside the game, and my ability to say fuck it—even when it meant walking away.

AWS re:invent was definitely the most fun hard work I had ever done, and I was never going to do it again. At the pinnacle of success, having run the impossible show, I knew I would be leaving the role and never putting myself through that again. The acclaim was not worth my health—both mental and physical—and not worth the time lost with my husband or my friends. I had done the impossible task because I have an inability to turn down a challenge, but now that the challenge had been completed what was left? I had a team I loved.

So why the hell am I telling you this strange mash up of stories about losing my best friend and a peak career moment? Because the event of losing someone so important to me had changed something in me on how I looked at the world, and even as I stood on that chair giving my speech to get everyone over the finish line, I knew I would never do launch for re:Invent again. In fact, I was thinking about leaving the company entirely. I had lost a lot of time with Kate because I was so busy with this job, and had continued to miss things that were important to me.

In private, I had joked with my husband about the song I would play as I quit at the end of the biggest keynote and walked out of the room. For the record, pulling a *Breakfast Club,* fist raised as I walked out to "Don't Forget About Me" had a slim lead over Queen's "I Want to Break Free." In reality, he and I had more than a few long talks over how work was going and what I wanted to do.

At the end of the day, there will be a time when, no matter how hard you fought, or how solid you are at the top of your game, that you need to look around and say fuck it, this is not worth it. It might not be worth the time away from your family; it might not be worth sitting on the floor of your bedroom sobbing into your dog's fur every morning before getting in the shower; it might not be worth having to fake a smile for just one more day. That better thing for you might be just over the horizon, but you have to be able to pick your head up and look.

Now is where we talk about how to decide if enough is enough.

1. Take a serious look at your finances to determine if you need to line up the next job before you quit the current one. This will map out your next moves.
2. Do a serious check in with your health. Have you been to the doctor more lately? Is your Apple watch constantly yelling at you for your heart rate being too high for someone sitting at a computer? Feeling exhausted and sick all the time isn't normal.
3. Do a serious check with your family. Have you been a dick lately? Your stress is likely impacting those who live with you, so check in with them.
4. Can you move somewhere else within the company where it is better?
5. If no, and you can financially support yourself for, at minimum, six months, fuck it, quit.

6. If no, and you need to find another job, first get that resume out there.

   a. Set aside one to two hours every day for job hunting and networking.

7. Draft your resignation letter. It's surprisingly therapeutic. I especially enjoyed telling ChatGPT to write resignation letters for me in the styles of Dr. Seuss. Let me share.

Oh, the Places I Won't Stay!

Dear [Supervisor's Name],
In this land of corporate whimsy, where dreams often roam,
I must tell you, with sadness, I'm no longer at home.
In the land of no goals, where leadership's amiss,
I've decided it's time for me to dismiss.
The Lorax once spoke for the trees with such might,
But here, in this office, there's no vision in sight.
No goals, no direction, like a Grinch's small heart,
It's time for me to make a fresh start.
Oh, the growth I had hoped for, like a seed in the ground,
But alas, it's not here, not a trace to be found.
No Horton to nurture and help it to grow,
In this place of stagnation, it's time to let go.
The toxicity lingers, like a Sneetch's green star,
Creating an environment that's truly bizarre.
Thank you for the memories, the lessons, and more,
But it's time to move on, to find what's in store.
Oh, the places I won't stay, with a heart light and free,
It's time for a new chapter, just watch and you'll see!
Sincerely,
[Your Name]

One way or another, if you spend every Sunday sick to your stomach about Monday, your family is avoiding you because of your mood, or you just hate life? Fuck it, my friend, fuck it. Take your talent and walk.

It is that simple. Notice I don't say easy. Nothing worth doing is easy. Nurture your talents and your innate sense of Fuck it, Watch This, at a place that deserves your effort. No company is "family" no matter what they say, and you will always be a cog in the wheel, but you get to decide what kind of cog you are and where you spend your energy. You have one life, put both middle fingers in the air and rock it.

CHAPTER 18

Mayday, Mayday

I know I just talked about quitting your job, and that most of this book is about the things you can do and the tactics you can use to get ahead. I wanted to end the book with the hardest thing you will ever do—the one that took me the longest to learn how to do. You need to know when to ask for help.

There are perceived social costs of asking for help, especially for men. A field study of physicians and nurses asking for help regarding a new computer system within a large hospital showed that individuals reported asking for help "... when they were male, in male-oriented occupations, and when the task was central to the organization's core competence."[1]

The same was true in the Coast Guard with officers. Even though lip service was given to "don't be a hero" and how asking for help when you didn't know how to do something was okay... it really wasn't. Asking for help because you were struggling mentally? While few people would say it outright, it was a career killer.

While you were not punished for asking for help, you were treated differently if you did. Leadership would start treating you like you were unreliable or had no clue what you were doing across the board. Sometimes your team would do the same. So instead of proactively asking for help, I learned to research quietly or mimic what I saw others do.

The stigma against asking for help was even more noticeable when it came to asking for help due to mental health issues, be it depression, anxiety, or any variety of neurodivergence struggles.

Finding an exact number for suicide rates in the Coast Guard is hard. Fun fact: they are not a part of the Annual Suicide Report the Department of Defense is required to do. The numbers from that report is 28.7 per 100,000 uniformed members.[2] I have lost three Coast Guard shipmates to suicide. Those are the ones that were confirmed suicides, not those that were the result of passive suicide ideation. Passive suicidal ideation is when a person thinks about or wishes for death without actually planning to end their life, so they show dangerous behaviors that can lead to death such as drinking and driving, riding a motorcycle at reckless speeds, and many other variations. Those deaths are marked as accidents, not suicides.

At a Coast Guard Foundation event I attended in 2023, the subject of suicide rates in the service came up. When I advocated to the admiral who was hosting the event that I strongly believed that a check-in with a mental health provider should be included as a part of the required annual wellness checks for service members, he chuckled. He told me that they already do a check-in.

This form, the Physical Health Assessment (PHA), is a check-the-box form[3] and includes questions like "Do you wear your seatbelt?"

When I said that no one is going to check a box on a form stating they have depression or suicidal thoughts because it could wreck their career, he gave me a response that was obviously meant to end the conversation.

"If I am willing to check a box that says I wear a condom when I have sex with my wife…"

I didn't let him finish. I told him that was not the same thing because it was not a career-ending question. His response was a clear example of leadership not only not understanding the breadth and depth of the mental health issues but their unwillingness to have a real conversation about it. I went on to detail that making a check-in with a mental health professional mandatory would begin the work of destigmatizing getting help and would help flag people who were at risk but too scared to come forward.

The admiral then went on to explain to me how there weren't enough mental health professionals working for the Coast Guard, and it was too expensive to do what I was suggesting because it would mean hiring contractors. That's right, this flag officer's response to my suggestion to help with the suicide problem wasn't that it wouldn't work; it was that it was too expensive.

GETTING HIT BY CARS

Is it any wonder, then, that it took me getting injured to finally go to a clinic in the Coast Guard for help? I was going through a nasty divorce and had recently been assaulted by someone I thought was a friend. On top of that, I was working in the command center I talked about earlier where I had no support from my peers or my executive officer (XO) when I asked for help. This XO was the one who also aggressively dismissed the reports from me and a few other women about an Auxiliarist—the Auxiliary is a volunteer organization that supports the service—for inappropriate behavior. An Auxiliarist who ended up being convicted of pedophilia and child pornography before my tour was over. So, as you can imagine, I was in a very bad, very dark place.

I was passively suicidal. While I wasn't plotting ways to take my life, I didn't care if something happened to me. I wasn't sleeping and had started drinking to avoid my problems. One day, I was hit by a car while walking in a crosswalk. I wasn't hit hard and came away from the incident with some intense bruises, but I was lucky. It was then a civilian friend told me she was worried about me. I can't thank you enough, Karianne.

So, I went to the clinic on base. I made the appointment under the request to talk about my Hashimoto's—an immune disorder that basically means my body attacks my thyroid—so there would be no documentation of what I actually wanted to talk to the doctor about. It took no time at all during the discussion with the physician for him to prescribe me an antidepressant and write a referral for a psychologist.

It is worth noting here that if you went through the employee assistance program at the time, you got a counselor, which is not the same at all. I started seeing the therapist and had a medical waiver I had to be given the time to see him at minimum once a week. This meant that my command had to know because my watch rotations had to be scheduled around this appointment.

My executive officer took it out on my Officer Evaluation Report (OER.) While the OER was not a bad one, it was what we call a plateau OER. He couldn't justify dropping my marks when he went to the command officer about it, so he gave me all the same marks I had had in the period before and wrote very passive-aggressive lackluster phrases in the report. This OER was the last one I had before I was up for the next rank since I was heading to graduate school, where you didn't do OERs; you had your grade reports. So I was punished for both needing and asking for help.

I continued to see a therapist while in graduate school, but while I was getting the mental health help I needed, I continued to avoid asking for help or showing any sort of struggle in the workplace. It wasn't until my best friend died in 2017 and I found out while I was at work that this all changed. It was kind of hard for people to not know I needed help when I collapsed sobbing in an empty office while on the phone.

The moment is pretty fuzzy, but I do remember one of my managers coming into the office, getting down on the floor with me, and asking if it was okay to hug me. He gently took my phone from me and told my friend's brother what was happening and that I would call him back, and called my mom and my now husband. He then ordered me a Lyft on his phone, and got one of my coworkers to ride home with me and stay with me until my husband arrived.

Then my direct manager checked in on me and let me know to take the week and check in the next week. Kate wasn't my blood family, but they treated the situation like I had lost a sister. Which, in my heart, I had. I was encouraged to work from home until I was ready. When I returned physically to the office, everyone was so kind.

This kindness without judgment changed my world. It changed how I saw being vulnerable at work.

I would love to say it changed how I handled needing help myself, but my burnout in 2020 landed me in the ER with heart problems that would indicate otherwise. I had gotten really good at asking for help when it came to learning things I didn't know at work and encouraged my people to ask for help, but I still struggled with giving myself a break. And break I did. So before leaving AWS, I took a medical leave of absence because my health had deteriorated enough that my heart was struggling. Luckily, again, I had an amazing manager who was super supportive both when I took the leave and when, at the end of that leave, I made the decision to not return.

According to the American Psychological Association, when stress is long term or chronic, it can have some serious effects on your body, and not just on one part. Chronic stress can impact your endocrine, gastrointestinal, nervous, reproductive, and musculoskeletal systems.[4] In my case, constant stress contributed to hypertension and my heart stuttering. So, even though I had learned a lot about help and kindness when Kate died, I still hadn't learned that I didn't need to take on everything all the time and live in a constant state of stress.

Constant stress can lead to burnout. Burnout is included in the 11th Revision of the International Classification of Diseases (ICD-11) as an occupational phenomenon. Burnout is defined in ICD-11 as follows:

"Burnout is a syndrome conceptualized as resulting from chronic workplace stress that has not been successfully managed. It is characterized by three dimensions:

- feelings of energy depletion or exhaustion;
- increased mental distance from one's job, or feelings of negativism or cynicism related to one's job; and
- reduced professional efficacy.

Burnout refers specifically to phenomena in the occupational context and should not be applied to describe experiences in other areas of life."[5]

So asking for help when your mental health being impacted is even more important than asking for task help. Jobs come and go; you only get one body and one life. The long-term impacts of toughing it out through burnout can quite literally ruin your life.

SUCK IT UP, BUTTERCUP

Suck up your pride, that is. Yeah, there will be leaders who look at you like you are weak or somehow less than for asking for help, or openly talking about mental health issues with others. In my last role, there were definitely issues with my manager around this. My team, on the other hand, deeply appreciated that I was open about having ADHD and CPTSD. More than once, I had a team member tell me it made them feel safe to take care of themselves.

Did my asking for help in the Coast Guard impact my career? Undeniably. Did it also impact me at my role as a VP at another company? Absolutely. Then again, I am healthier, happier, and successful. My people felt seen and supported too, so my being openly vulnerable and honest helped others. To me, those are the real wins.

Frankly? Fuck working for a company where being neurodivergent, having a disability, or asking for help due to burnout results in being punished or retaliated against. While there are laws against discrimination for medical reasons, it does still happen. So what do you do?

Document everything. Get documentation from your doctors if it gets that far along. Keep emails, notes, or anything else from meetings if managers say anything inappropriate. I had a manager tell me "I got sick all the time"—after I got COVID-19 and then a sinus infection, by the way. He also responded poorly when I asked for some accommodations. Specifically, I had two medical—one physical and one mental—appointments a week that I could not move or miss.

It is both better for my career and my health to never work with this person again.

All right, so document everything is kind of obvious, but how do you know when to ask for help, and how do you actually do it?

- Start by checking in with your friends and family. Are you acting differently, maybe more irritable, tired all the time?
- Look at your health. Has your blood pressure gone up? Do you have frequent headaches? Trouble sleeping?
- Find forms—no, not the ones on Facebook. like the publicly available PHQ-9 (Patient Health Question for Depression) or the GAD-7 (General Anxiety) and check your results.

If you hear from your loved ones that they are worried or think you are burning the candle at both ends, or you see signs in your health changes, or the forms give you concerning scores, you need to ask for help. If you are unsure whether you need to ask for help, ask for help.

Asking for help comes in many forms.

- Let your loved ones know you are struggling and could use extra support.
- Check with your company what confidential employee assistance options there are.
- Check your medical insurance to see what your options are for finding a therapist.

- If you need to take time off, check your company's medical leave policy, and remember, mental health is medical too.
- Don't be afraid of medication. Just because you need a medical boost to help doesn't mean you are less than or weak.

Remember, a big part of saying fuck it, watch this is to triumph over the hardest times. The hardest situation you are likely to face is speaking up when you need help, be it for physical or mental health, because you are being harassed, or because you just need to learn how to do something new. It is in your future you's best interest to suck up your pride and raise your hand for that help.

Beyond that, the people who work with you and work for you will gain courage from you showing the courage needed to be vulnerable and real. You are more important than any project, any job, or any shitty manager's opinion of you. No matter how many times you say fuck it to everything else, you should never say fuck it to your well-being.

Acknowledgments

This might be the hardest part of the book to write—after the ask-for-help chapter—because I am so worried I am going to miss someone.

First, I want to thank my husband, Eric, for the loving, gentle nudges to get off my ass and write a book about all of this. I couldn't have done this—this being all the things: the book, my own business, etc.—without your love and support.

Then there is the Lady Cabal—Cheryl, Kristal, Jam, Chelsea, Nora, and Emily. I am so lucky to have such fierce badass women in my life. You have been there with me through everything and are the sisters of my heart. You cheered me on through this entire process, just like you have every challenge I faced, and I can't thank you enough.

Of course, I need to thank my parents. Dad, thank you for the career advice you gave me and for not taking it personally when I ignored most of it and did things that made you think I was crazy. We haven't always seen eye to eye, but I cherish the friendship we have built. Mom, thank you for showing me that Fuck It is a way to do things. You never turned away from a challenge, especially when the good old boys' club said you couldn't do something because you were a woman. Growing up with you as an example helped me be who I am today.

Captains Diane Durham and Steve Krupa, you are more than officers I looked up to when I was in; you have been family since I was a little kid. Captain Greg Stanclik, dziękuję for making me a Polar Bear and for being such an incredible leader and friend. Admiral Joel Whitehead, thank you for taking a chance on a young ensign to be your PAO. CDR Krystyn Pecora for being a partner in mischief and chaos coordination.

Jeff Barr and Neil Davey, the two of you have been encouraging me to get to writing for years. Thank you. Yes, you were right. Shannon Loftis, thank you for your help reading, and for being the best big sister and mentor ever.

Of course, I would be remiss if I didn't thank Erinn Kemper, my editor, for her hard work helping this book come to life, and my beta readers.

To my teams: not only was it amazing to work with all of you, but you humbled me—and maybe made me cry—with how you have kept in touch since we parted ways. There is no bigger honor than your support even after we have all moved on to new jobs.

Then of course I need to thank all the people who backed getting this book published: Jamileh Delcambre, Kristal DeCoux, Amye Scavarda Perrin, Terry Holloway, Roger

Neustadter, Jeff Barr, Andrea Vinyard, Matthew Harmon, Steve Syfuhs, Dave Visneski, C.C.Chapman, Adam Daigle, Kristin Hamilton, Samuel Richard, Joel Emans, Ted Ellis, Todd Barr, Sharon Fetter, Thomas Roberts, Daniel Westermann-Clark, Kenneth Leung, Sean Plankey, Joe Reitz, Regina Caffrey, Bo English-Wiczling, Adrian Hornsby, Veronica Steele, Kevin Goddard, Meg Rapelye, Nora Guzman, Richelle Bixler, Daniel Helmick, Philip Fitzsimons, Eric Koester, Russell Hall, Karl Spang, Rick Timkovich, Patrik Zuest, Krystyn Pecora, Jessica Hall, Shannon Loftis, Darlyn Harrell, Phil Curran, Kellsey Ruppel, Daren Lewis, Rob Nolen, Rahul Pathak, Isa Mariano, Arthur F. Tyde III, Nate Ferrell, Tim Shea, Christopher O'Neil, Dan Head, Mike Selinker, Marika VanderSmith, Marlo Straub, Aaron Liao, Donnaann Visneski, Jamie Rehberg, John Kovalic, Lindsay Hua, Brandi Murphy, Kimberly Smith, Zac Crawford, Paul Roszkowski, Guy Langman, Mishi Schueller, Lee Terrill, Heather Werckle, Emily Titcomb, Dominic Catalano, Rob Dolin, Eric Neustadter, Linda Naugle, Ashley Long, Stefany Martin, Tyler Schroder, Amanda Powter, Chris Langston, Lori Visneski- Fink, Monique Priestley, Staten Hansen, Dan Donovan, Philippe-Antoine Menard, Justin Stanley, Thomas Diamond, Christine Lawrence, Colin VanderSmith, Anne Pelz, Benjamin Janczyk, Albert Yao, Michael Ender, Jessica Keele, Kellie Caron, Shannon Riley, Glenn White.

Thanks to you readers, this wasn't the first book I planned to write (I thought it was going to be a horror novel!), but as I hope you have learned reading this collection of sea stories... gotta adapt to the moment and just go with it!

APPENDIX

CHAPTER 2

1. William Storr, *The Status Game* (New York: Harper Collins, 2021).

CHAPTER 3

1. *UKG Global Survey 2023-Manager Impact on Mental Health* (UKG Inc, 2023). www.ukg.com/sites/default/files/2023-01/CV2040-Part2-UKG%20Global%20Survey%202023-Manager%20Impact%20on%20Mental%20Health-Final.pdf

2. Jackie Wiles, "Think Employees Thrive with Constant Coaching? Think Again," Gartner.com, last modified July 25, 2019, https://www.gartner.com/smarterwithgartner/think-employees-thrive-with-constant-coaching-think-again.

CHAPTER 4

1. Karen Huang, Michael Yeomans, Alison Wood Brooks, Julia Minson, and Francesca Gino, "It Doesn't Hurt to Ask: Question-Asking Increases Liking," *Journal of Personality and Social Psychology* Volume 11, no. 3

(November 2017) 430–452, https://www.hbs.edu/ris/Publication%20Files/Huang%20et%20al%202017_6945bc5e-3b3e-4c0a-addd-254c9e603c60.pdf.

2. Ashley Feinberg, "11 of the Most Embarrassing Government Websites," Gizmodo, last modified August 12, 2014, https://gizmodo.com/11-of-the-most-embarrassing-government-websites-1619676187.

CHAPTER 5

1. United Nations Educational, Scientific and Cultural Organization, "Global Ocean Science Report 2020: Charting Capacity for Ocean Sustainability." Global Ocean Science Report 2020, Page 21–42.

2. James Clear, *Atomic Habits: An Easy & Proven Way to Build Good Habits & Break Bad Ones.* (New York: Penguin Random House, 2018).

CHAPTER 6

1. Elizabeth Schrauben, "Communication in Crisis: An Analysis of the Role Organizational Structures Play in the Effectiveness of Crisis Communication," (Presentation at Grand Valley State University, October 19, 2011).

CHAPTER 7

1. Morley Safer, "Dolly Parton: The Real Queen of All Media," *60 Minutes*, April 2, 2009, last modified June 9, 2009, https://www.cbsnews.com/news/dolly-parton-the-real-queen-of-all-media/.

2. Fiona E. Murray, "Faculty as Catalysts for Training New Inventors: Differential Outcomes for Male and Female PhD Students," *PNAS* 120, no. 36 (June 15, 2022).

3. Morley Safer, "Dolly Parton: The Real Queen of All Media," *60 Minutes*, April 2, 2009, last modified June 9, 2009, https://www.cbsnews.com/news/dolly-parton-the-real-queen-of-all-media/.

4. Courtney Connley, "From the U.S. Coast Guard to a VP at Oracle: How This Executive Charted Her Own Path into Tech," Chief, last modified April 20, 2023. https://chief.com/articles/from-the-us-coast-guard-to-vp-at-oracle-how-this-executive-chartered-her-own-path-into-tech.

CHAPTER 8

1. Morgan Winsor, "A Timeline of the Missing Titanic Tourist Submersible," ABC News, last modified June 27, 2023, https://abcnews.go.com/International/missing-titanic-tourist-submersible-timeline/story?id=100265183.

2. Alex Kantrowitz, "My Experience Aboard the OceanGate Sub—With David Pogue of CBS," YouTube Alex Kantrowitz, July 27, 2023, 43:49, https://www.youtube.com/watch?v=WcEjISrdQl4.

3. *Oceangate v. David Lochridge*, 123 F. Supp. 456 (District Court 2022).

4. PA2 Nyxolyno Cangemi, "Hacking, Smashing, and Dashing," *Coast Guard Magazine*, Special Edition 2005.

CHAPTER 9

1. M. F. McAllister, *"Fouled Anchor" Investigation—Final Report*, Ref: (a) DCMS-D memo 5800 dated 8 Nov 2018 (Interim Report). https://www.uscg.mil/Portals/0/documents/

FOULED_ANCHOR_INVESTIGATION_FINAL_
REPORT_AND_ENCLOSURE-508Compliant.pdf

2. Letter from Congress to Admiral Linda L. Fagan, Commandant, U.S. Coast Guard, July 13, 2023. https://oversightdemocrats.house.gov/sites/democrats.oversight.house.gov/files/2023-07-13.JBR%20Thompson%20to%20Fagan-USCG%20re%20Fouled%20Anchor.pdf

3. Letter from Congress to Admiral Linda L. Fagan, Commandant, U.S. Coast Guard, July 13, 2023, https://oversightdemocrats.house.gov/sites/democrats.oversight.house.gov/files/2023-07-13.JBR%20Thompson%20to%20Fagan-USCG%20re%20Fouled%20Anchor.pdf.

4. Melissa K. McCafferty "Testimony of Melissa K. McCafferty," U.S. Senate Committee on Homeland Security and Government Affairs, Permanent Subcommittee on Investigations. December 12, 2023.

5. David Owen, CH FRCP, "Hubris Syndrome," *2008 Royal College of Physicians Clinical Medicine Vol 8 No 4 August 200*

6. Yi Tang, Jiatao Li, and Hongyan Yang, "What I See, What I Do: How Executive Hubris Affects Firm Innovation," *Sage Journals* 41, no. 6 (April 17, 2023): https://journals.sagepub.com/doi/10.1177/0149206312441211.

CHAPTER 10

1. United States Code of Federal Regulation 46 USCG 8104(b https://www.ecfr.gov/current/title-46/chapter-I/subchapter-B/part-15/subpart-G/section-15.705

CHAPTER 11

1. "Coast Guard Health Records: Timely Acquisition of New System Is Critical to Overcoming Challenges with

Paper Process," Report to Congressional Requesters, GAO-18–59 (January 2018). https://www.gao.gov/products/gao-18-59.

2. Department of Transportation, Federal Aviation Administration, *14 CFR part 93*, "Staffing Related Relief Concerning Operations at Ronald Reagan Washington National Airport, John F. Kennedy International Airport, LaGuardia Airport, and Newark Liberty International Airport," May 15, 2023, through September 15, 2023.

3. Sohail Husain, "Air Traffic Control Shortages and the Need for Reform," *Eno Center for Transportation*, August 18, 2023, https://enotrans.org/article/air-traffic-control-shortages-and-the-need-for-reform/.

4. Billy Nolen, Acting Administrator, Federal Aviation Administration, "The Federal Aviation Administration's NOTAM System Failure and its Impacts on a Resilient National Airspace," (Statement before the United States Senate Committee on Commerce, Science, and Transportation, Hearing on Notice to Air Missions System, February 15, 2023).

5. "FAA Faces Controller Staffing Challenges as Air Traffic Operations Return to Pre-Pandemic Levels at Critical Facilities," Self-Initiated Report, Federal Aviation Administration, AV2023035, June 21, 2023

CHAPTER 12

1. University of Essex, "All Work and No Play Will Really Make a Dull Life," *Medical Xpress*, (September 14, 2023), https://medicalxpress.com/news/2023-09-play-life-dull-reveals.html.

2. University of Sydney, "Benefits of Team Building Exercises Jeopardized If Not Truly Voluntary,"

ScienceDaily, February 25, 2021, https://www.sciencedaily. com/releases/2021/02/210225143709.htm#.

CHAPTER 13

1. Kyle Orland, "E3 is Officially Dead, and So Is the Version of the Industry It Was Made For," Ars Technica, Updated Dec. 12, 2023 https://arstechnica.com/gaming/2023/12/ how-the-internet-killed-e3/

2. *Cambridge Dictionary* (Cambridge, UK: Cambridge University Press, 2024), s.v. "Crunch." https://dictionary. cambridge.org/us/dictionary/english/crunch.

3. Johanna Weststar, Eva Kwan, and Shruti Kumar, "Developer Satisfaction Survey 2019: Summary Report" (Sacramento, California, International Game Developers Association, 2019).

4. Jason Schreier, "Video Game Industry Still Has Much to Learn About Excessive Overtime," Bloomberg, September 9, 2022, https://www.bloomberg.com/news/ newsletters/2022-09-09/video-game-executive-faces- backlash-over-comments-about-crunch.

CHAPTER 15

1. T. A. Ito, J. T. Larsen, N. K. Smith, and J. T. Cacioppo, "Negative Information Weighs More Heavily on the Brain: The Negativity Bias in Evaluative Categorizations," *Journal of Personality and Social Psychology* 75, no. 4 (2016): 887–900, https://doi.org/10.1037/0022-3514.75.4.887.

CHAPTER 16

1. The National Institute for Occupational Safety and Health, "Stress…At Work," publication number 99–101,

September 12, 2023, https://www.cdc.gov/niosh/docs/99-101/default.html.

CHAPTER 18

1. Fiona Lee, "The Social Costs of Seeking Help," *Journal of Applied Psychology* 38, no. 1 (March 2002): https://doi.org/10.1177/0021886302381002.
2. *The Department of Defense Annual Suicide Report (ASR) 2002.*
3. U.S. Coast Guard, "PHA Instructions," accessed November 2023, https://www.dcms.uscg.mil/Portals/10/DOL/BaseNCR/doc/PHA_Instructions.pdf.
4. "Research Findings on Stress." American Psychological Association. Accessed February 14, 2024. https://www.apa.org/topics/stress/research-findings.
5. International Classification of Diseases, 11th Revision (ICD-11). Geneva: World Health Organization, 2018. Accessed February 14, 2024. https://icd.who.int/browse11/l-m/en.